3

68

TREES

EDITED BY

JILL FAIRCHILD

Weidenfeld & Nicolson

New York

TREES

A CELEBRATION

Published by Weidenfeld & Nicolson
A division of Wheatland Corporation
841 Broadway
New York, NY 10003-4793

Published in Canada by General Publishing Company, Ltd.

Due to limitations of space, permissions appear on page 113.

Library of Congress Cataloging-in-Publication Data
Trees: a celebration / edited by Jill Fairchild.—1st ed.
ISBN 1-55584-313-1
1. *Trees—Literary collections.   I. Fairchild, Jill, 1926–*
PN6071.T74V34   1989
808.8'036—dc19   89-30830
CIP

Manufactured in the United States of America
This book is printed on acid-free paper
Designed by Cynthia Krupat
First Edition 1989
1 3 5 7 9 10 8 6 4 2

To my husband John

and my children John, James, Jill, and Stephen

Contents

Contents

Contents

Contents

Contents

Preface

This little book is dedicated to trees all over the world. Its existence is the result of my concern for the plight of trees on this Earth. Rather than desecrate them as man is doing all over this planet, it seemed fitting to celebrate their being. Trees are a necessity to life, for without them we would not have air to breathe, food to eat, water to drink, medicines, shelter, nor shade. Trees stop erosion, halt floods and droughts, release oxygen, and harness the sun's energy, which in turn enables us to live through and by them.

But trees also nurture the soul—they inspire thought and meditation. We all need to be inspired by beauty, and for centuries writers all over the world have found meaning in trees—they seemed to symbolize the human spirit and showed how nature transcends man. This volume collects some of those writers' works; it is a very personal anthology, but I hope it will be a good companion at all times to all people.

I want to thank John Saumarez-Smith for his invaluable help in editing the selections, and Dr. Jurg Stahel for his help and enthusiasm, and for being a guardian of the forest.

TREES

L. F. JEHAN

The Creation

Then shall all the trees of the wood

rejoice before the Lord.

(Psalm 96, 12, 13)

What place in the world is more magnificent and more imposing than a vast beautiful forest! Its tree trunks, such as those of the beeches and the firs, surpass in beauty and height the most majestic columns; its verdant vaults exceed in grace and audacity those of our monuments. In the daytime, the sun's rays penetrate its dense foliage and, passing through a thousand verdant hues, paint the earth with shadows mingled with light. At night, the heavenly bodies can be perceived rising here and there above the treetops, as if they were bearing stars in their branches: it is an august temple that has its columns, its porticos, its sanctuaries and its lamps. This immense edifice is mobile; the wind blows, the rustling of the leaves mingles with the diverse songs of the birds, and from afar, the swaying tree trunks are heard as religious murmurs that incline the soul to meditation, and fill it with a feeling of love and admiration for the Divinity revealed by this solemn spectacle.

In its primitive state, the earth offered only three great sources of life: those of the forests, of the meadows, and of the waters. In these three spheres, linked by reciprocal harmonies of dependence, such an immensity of beings and productions is sown that the centuries will never be able to enumerate them, or know them all. To describe their number, their mechanism, and their perfection is beyond the compass of human nature; the greatest, the most sublime geniuses humble themselves, like so many Newtons, at the feet of that Omnipotence, which could not be penetrated by all the great minds in the world put together, who can only worship Him and give thanks for His blessings.

If a landscape without water is a fairy palace without mirrors, we may say that a terrain without landscape is a disenchanted region. Woods, which so agreeably delight and rest the eyes, and allow their beautiful undulations of varied verdure to blend so gracefully the brilliant colours of the sky with the azure undulations of the waters, form a whole that offers all the harmonies possible to increase the charm and joy of life. In their warm, tranquil enclosure, nature covers herself with an abundance of flowers; and the sweet-smelling and medicinal plants that grow there in profusion are more perfect than anywhere else. For woods are, by their nature and their continual movement, the ventilators of the earth, and spread its aromatics and its health-giving virtues wherever man must breathe them. If we consider that one single leaf of a beech, of an oak, or of a walnut, has more than a hundred thousand pores with which to breathe in and breathe out the air charged with terrestrial vapours and emanations, we may form an idea of the influence great masses of trees may exert on the animal economy by their suction and transpiration.

If trees in small masses have the harmonic virtue of imitating with their rustling the murmur and fall of water, great forests also, soaring up into the skies and designed to break the violence of the winds, reproduce with their solemn, uniform undulations the imposing sound of the sea's rolling waves. It is in an area of dense afforestation, where all the elements have a tongue to interpret the mysteries of nature, that we hear in the air, on the waters, or in the recesses of the rocks, voices calling, and voices responding. We may say of a forest that there are as many different voices as there are leaves, so much do the sounds echo one another and multiply under those sonorous vaults of verdure. Of all the living scenes that enchant us with every step we take in these refuges, in which all our sensations are different from those we experience in open country, the most imposing is that of electrical meteorites.

No sooner does the sound of thunder begin to make itself heard than the birdsong ceases; a profound silence follows the universal joy, one suddenly seems to be alone in the world; all one hears, all one sees, is the soft vibration of the leaves; it seems that all nature is stilling her voice in order to hear, in terror, that resounding voice, which silences all others. Nowhere has the thunder such resonance as in a forest. Its prolonged rolls, long-repeated in the most imposing fashion, awaken a profoundly religious feeling. Each clangour produces a general tremor among all the foliage. Here one feels that in response to this voice from Mount Sinai, whose effect is beyond all expression, nature in her entirety is shaken and suppliant at the feet of one of the Lord's great powers.

But trees are not merely designed to be the most beautiful adornment of the countryside, to embellish man's dwelling place, to provide him with delightful coolness under their shade during the heat of summer; above all they offer him endless resources of comforts and amenities because of the great number of uses he puts them to. We cannot take a step in our factories, our workshops, or even our houses, without perceiving a whole host of products due to man's industry, whose material has been taken from the plant kingdom. These beings who, during their lifetime, have peopled the countryside and the forests, are taken after their death to the villages and the towns, where some are used in the construction of buildings, others converted into garments, and most are transformed into furniture, into utensils of all kinds, as useful as they are convenient. The table that serves for our meals, the bed upon which we repose, the doors that ensure our tranquility, the coffers and caskets in which we deposit our gold and our papers, the barrels that conserve our food and drink, the carriages that transport us, the vessels that distribute our resources throughout the two worlds, the colours with which our fabrics are dyed, those that depict us on ivory or canvas, all these things and an infinity of others are so many blessings of nature's most agreeable kingdom. Thus the destruction, or rather the use, of plants nourishes a great number of arts, be they of prime necessity or of luxury, and these bodies, although deprived of life, yield under the hand of man to all the forms he wishes to give them and to all the uses he demands of them. It is also from the heart of these plants, dead and consumed by fire, that in winter we draw the warmth we lack; and when that melancholy season is over, it is with plants fashioned into instruments that we celebrate the return of the spring and the flowers.

Before they are delivered up to the axe, however, how many presents have trees not made us! It is from their branches that the apple and the orange fall at our feet: the ones give us a fruit that takes the place of bread; others provide us with a vinous liquor; chestnuts and sweet acorns contain a kind of flour; sago comes from the pith of a palm tree; oil flows from the olive tree, the walnut tree, the beech tree; the sap of the birch is a refreshing liquor; the leaves of the talipot and the banana tree are used to thatch huts; ropes are made from the bark of the lime tree, from the *Antidesme* and from one of the gum trees, and fabric from the bark of several others. The leaves of the mulberry are woven with silk; sugar is extracted from the sap of the maples; resin and turpentine exude from the bark of the firs and the terebinths: the seed of several myrtles is enveloped in wax; a Chinese tree produces tallow; varnishes come out of the trunk of the Japanese lacquer tree; manna solidifies on the leaves of the ash and the larch, at whose feet grows the medicinal agaric; the acid sap of the tamarind counteracts noisome humours; the cassia furnishes a mild soothing laxative; the bark of the cinchonas (the Quinquinas) quells fevers; the poplar and the copaiba yield a cleansing balsam; the guiacum performs the miracles of mercury. We should never come to an end were we to wish to enumerate all the uses of the vegetable kingdom. Such is the profusion of nature, that she frequently gathers together in a single one of her productions the advantages of all the others.

Woods and forests exist in all countries and in all latitudes. The basins formed by mountain chains, the lofty peaks of the Alps and the Cordilleras, the deserts of Siberia, the shores laved by the Ganges or the Caspian sea, the burning coasts of Africa, the vast swamps bordering the lakes and great rivers of South America, the numerous islands thrown up as if by chance in the Southern seas or grouped together in the archi-pelagos of Mexico and the Indies—all these different countries are covered with woods, whose expanse, whether greater or smaller, is almost always in inverse ratio to man's needs. This disproportion is not nature's fault, but that of man who, when in the savage state, entertains for the forests that have known him from birth a childlike respect maintained by his idleness, but who on the contrary, when in a state of civilization, is either so anxious to consume or so tormented by his insatiable cupidity that he has no respect for anything, and with a disas-trous, murderous hand fells all the woods that surround him and in a single day destroys the work of several centuries.

Thus, as the inhabitants of a country become more enlightened, more active and more industrious, which is to say more avid of every kind of pleasure, the number and the extent of the forests in that country must necessarily diminish. That is why England no longer has any at all, and why France today has so few that we may compare them to those that existed here in the days of Caesar. Most of them, it will be said, have been converted into fields sown with grain, into valuable vineyards, or into pastures that nourish innumerable herds. That is true. But how many millions of trees has our frantic search for luxury not destroyed? How many does it not destroy every year, while almost nobody takes the trouble to replace even a part of them? In former times, one single fire sufficed for a whole family, which thereby lived a more united and happier life. Today, egotism and vanity isolate everyone, and in the house of a simple citizen we see almost as many fires as individuals. When we add to this the enormous quantity of wood that is burned, not only in every type of administrative office necessitated by the business of government, but also in places of entertainment, cafes, clubs, and a host of similar establishments maintained by want of occupation and multiplied to the point of satiety, then we will no doubt be amazed that what remains to us of our ancient forests can provide for such consumption. However liberal and even prodigal nature shows herself to us in the reproduction of her woods, we are even more prodigal than she, and we shall soon find a way to exhaust the resources she offers us, for the harm we do is continually on the increase.

If we deign to consider that a single family of trees is a habitat for numerous tribes who successively find in it their cradle, their pasture, and their shelter, and that similar habitats, multiplied by the infinite diversity of the vegetable kingdom, harbour in their midst an immense series of beings, from the stag, the pride of the forests, to the industrious bee; from the noisy capercaillie, which celebrates the matutinal dawn, to the melodious songster of the coppices, which renders melodious even the silence of the night; from the menacing buzzard to the timorous dove; and so on; we can understand that whenever a wood is felled, a void is produced in life and in the harmony of nature, and that the more wood we destroy, the more we restrict the circle of so many existences which were designed to animate the earth, the air and the water with their indefinable charm, whose united concert of voices, of productions, of adornments, and of grandeurs of all descriptions should be the fulfillment and delight of man!

Translated by Barbara Woijlrt

JOHN FOWLES

FROM *The Tree*

More and more I secretly craved everything our own environment did not possess—space, wildness, hills, woods. I think especially woodland, "real" trees. With one or two exceptions—the Essex Marshlands, Arctic tundra—I have always loathed flat and treeless country. Time there seems to dominate, it ticks remorselessly like a clock. But trees warp time, or rather create a variety of times—here dense and abrupt, there calm and sinuous—never plodding, mechanical, inescapably monotonous. I still feel this as soon as I enter one of the countless secret little woods in the Devon-Dorset border country where I now live. It is almost like leaving land to go into water—another medium, another dimension. When I was younger, this sensation was acute. Slinking into trees was always slinking into heaven. . . .

In a wood the actual visual "frontier" of any one tree is usually impossible to distinguish—at least in summer. We feel or think we feel nearest to a tree's "essence" (or that of its species) when it chances to stand like us, in isolation, but evolution did not intend trees to grow singly. Far more than ourselves, they are social creatures, and no more natural as isolated specimens than man is as a marooned sailor or hermit. Their society in turn creates or supports other societies of plants, insects, birds, mammals, micro organisms: all of which may choose to isolate and section off but which remain no less the ideal entity or the whole experience, of the wood— and indeed, are still so seen by most of primitive mankind. . . . The true wood, the true place of any kind is the sum of all its phenomena.

JEAN GIONO

The Man Who Planted Trees

For a human character to reveal truly exceptional qualities, one must have the good fortune to be able to observe its performance over many years. If this performance is devoid of all egoism, if its guiding motive is unparalleled generosity, if it is absolutely certain that there is no thought of recompense and that, in addition, it has left its visible mark upon the earth, then there can be no mistake.

About forty years ago I was taking a long trip on foot over mountain heights quite unknown to tourists, in that ancient region where the Alps thrust down into Provence. All this, at the time I embarked upon my long walk through these deserted regions, was barren and colorless land. Nothing grew there but wild lavender.

I was crossing the area at its widest point, and after three days' walking, found myself in the midst of unparalleled desolation. I camped near the vestiges of an abandoned village. I had run out of water the day before, and had to find some. These clustered houses, although in ruins, like an old wasps' nest, suggested that there must once have been a spring or well here. There was indeed a spring, but it was dry. The five or six houses, roofless, gnawed by wind and rain, the tiny chapel with its crumbling steeple, stood about like the houses and chapels in living villages, but all life had vanished.

It was a fine June day, brilliant with sunlight, but over this unsheltered land, high in the sky, the wind blew with unendurable ferocity. It growled over the carcasses of the houses like a lion disturbed at its meal. I had to move my camp.

After five hours' walking I had still not found water and there was nothing to give me any hope of finding any. All about me was the same dryness, the same coarse grasses. I thought I glimpsed in the distance a small black silhouette, upright, and took it for the trunk of a solitary tree. In any case I started toward it. It was a shepherd. Thirty sheep were lying about him on the baking earth.

He gave me a drink from his water-gourd and, a little later, took me to his cottage in a fold of the plain. He drew his water—excellent water—from a very deep natural well above which he had constructed a primitive winch.

The man spoke little. This is the way of those who live alone, but one felt that he was sure of himself, and confident in his assurance. That was unexpected in this barren country. He lived, not in a cabin, but in a real house built of stone that bore plain evidence of how his own efforts had reclaimed the ruin he had found there on his arrival. His roof was strong and sound. The wind on its tiles made the sound of the sea upon its shore.

The place was in order, the dishes washed, the floor swept, his rifle oiled; his soup was boiling over the fire. I noticed then that he was cleanly shaved, that all his buttons were firmly sewed on, that his clothing had been mended with the meticulous care that makes the mending invisible. He shared his soup with me and afterwards, when I offered my tobacco pouch, he told me that he did not smoke. His dog, as silent as himself, was friendly without being servile.

It was understood from the first that I should spend the night there; the nearest village was still more than a day and a half away. And besides I was perfectly familiar with the nature of the rare villages in that region. There were four or five of them scattered well apart from each other on these mountain slopes, among white oak thickets, at the extreme end of the wagon roads. They were inhabited by charcoalburners, and the living was bad. Families, crowded together in a climate that is excessively harsh both in winter and in summer found no escape from the unceasing conflict of personalities. Irrational ambition reached inordinate proportions in the continual desire for escape. The men took their wagonloads of charcoal to the town, then returned. The soundest characters broke under the perpetual grind. The women nursed their grievances. There was rivalry in everything, over the price of charcoal as over a pew in the church, over warring virtues as over warring vices as well as over the ceaseless combat between virtue and vice. And over all there was the wind, also ceaseless, to rasp upon the nerves. There were epidemics of suicide and frequent cases of insanity, usually homicidal.

The shepherd went to fetch a small sack and poured out a heap of acorns on the table. He began to inspect them, one by one, with great concentration, separating the good from the bad. I smoked my pipe. I did offer to help him. He told me that it was his job. And in fact, seeing the care he devoted to the task, I did not insist. That was the whole of our conversation. When he had set aside a large enough pile of good acorns he counted them out by tens, meanwhile eliminating the small ones or those which were slightly cracked, for now he examined them more closely. When he had thus selected one hundred perfect acorns he stopped and we went to bed.

There was peace in being with this man. The next day I asked if I might rest here for a day. He found it quite natural—or, to be more exact, he gave me the impression that nothing could startle him. The rest was not absolutely necessary, but I was interested and wished to know about him. He opened the pen and led his flock to pasture. Before leaving, he plunged his sack of carefully selected and counted acorns into a pail of water.

I noticed that he carried for a stick an iron rod as thick as my thumb and about a yard and a half long. Resting myself by walking, I followed a path parallel to his. His pasture was in a valley. He left the dog in charge of the little flock and climbed toward where I stood. I was afraid that he was about to rebuke me for my indiscretion, but it was not that at all: this was the way he was going, and he invited me to go along if I had nothing better to do. He climbed to the top of the ridge, about a hundred yards away.

There he began thrusting his iron rod into the earth, making a hole in which he planted an acorn; then he refilled the hole. He was planting oak trees. I asked him if the land belonged to him. He answered no. Did he know whose it was? He did not. He supposed it was community property, or perhaps belonged to people who cared nothing about it. He was not interested in finding out whose it was. He planted his hundred acorns with the greatest care.

After the midday meal he resumed his planting. I suppose I must have been fairly insistent in my questioning, for he answered me. For three years he had been planting trees in this wilderness. He had planted one hundred thousand. Of the hundred thousand, twenty thousand had sprouted. Of the twenty thousand he still expected to lose about half, to rodents or to the unpredictable designs of Providence. There remained ten thousand oak trees to grow where nothing had grown before.

That was when I began to wonder about the age of this man. He was obviously over fifty. Fifty-five, he told me. His name was Elzeard Bouffier. He had once had a farm in the lowlands. There he had had his life. He had lost his only son, then his wife. He had withdrawn into this solitude where his pleasure was to live leisurely with his lambs and his dog. It was his opinion that this land was dying for want of trees. He added that, having no very pressing business of his own, he had resolved to remedy this state of affairs.

Since I was at that time, in spite of my youth, leading a solitary life, I understood how to deal gently with solitary spirits. But my very youth forced me to consider the future in relation to myself and to a certain quest for happiness. I told him that in thirty years his ten thousand oaks would be magnificent. He answered quite simply that if God granted him life, in thirty years he would have planted so many more that these ten thousand would be like a drop of water in the ocean.

Besides, he was now studying the reproduction of beech trees and had a nursery of seedlings grown from beechnuts near his cottage. The seedlings, which he had protected from his sheep with a wire fence, were very beautiful. He was also considering birches for the valleys where, he told me, there was a certain amount of moisture a few yards below the surface of the soil.

The next day, we parted.

The following year came the War of 1914, in which I was involved for the next five years. An infantryman hardly had time for reflecting upon trees. To tell the truth, the thing itself had made no impression upon me; I had considered it as a hobby, a stamp collection, and forgotten it.

The war over, I found myself possessed of a tiny demobilization bonus and a huge desire to breathe fresh air for a while. It was with no other objective that I again took the road to the barren lands.

The countryside had not changed. However, beyond the deserted village I glimpsed in the distance a sort of greyish mist that covered the mountaintops like a carpet. Since the day before, I had begun to think again of the shepherd tree-planter. "Ten thousand oaks," I reflected, "really take up quite a bit of space."

I had seen too many men die during those five years not to imagine easily that Elzeard Bouffier was dead, especially since, at twenty, one regards men of fifty as old men with nothing left to do but die. He was not dead. As a matter of fact, he was extremely spry. He had changed jobs. Now he had only four sheep but, instead a hundred beehives. He had got rid of the sheep because they threatened his young trees. For, he told me (and I saw for myself), the war had disturbed him not at all. He had imperturbably continued to plant.

The oaks of 1910 were then ten years old and taller than either of us. It was an impressive spectacle. I was literally speechless and, as he did not talk, we spent the whole day walking in silence through his forest. In three sections, it measured eleven kilometers in length and three kilometers at its greatest width. When you remembered that all this had sprung from the hands and the soul of this one man, without technical resources, you understood that men could be as effectual as God in other realms than that of destruction.

He had pursued his plan, and beech trees as high as my shoulder, spreading out as far as the eye could reach, confirmed it. He showed me handsome clumps of birch planted five years before—that is, in 1915, when I had been fighting at Verdun. He had set them out in all the valleys where he had guessed—and rightly—that there was moisture almost at the surface of the ground. They were as delicate as young girls, and very well established.

Creation seemed to come about in a sort of chain reaction. He did not worry about it; he was determinedly pursuing his task in all its simplicity; but as we went back toward the village I saw water flowing in brooks that had been dry since the memory of man. This was the most impressive result of chain reaction that I had seen. These dry streams had once, long ago, run with water. Some of the dreary villages I mentioned before had been built on the sites of ancient Roman settlements, traces of which still remained; and archaeologists, exploring there, had found fishhooks where, in the twentieth century, cisterns were needed to assure a small supply of water.

The wind, too, scattered seeds. As the water reappeared, so there reappeared willows, rushes, meadows, gardens, flowers, and a certain purpose in being alive. But the transformation took place so gradually that it became a part of the pattern without causing any astonishment. Hunters, climbing into the wilderness in pursuit of hares or wild boar, had of course noticed the sudden growth of little trees, but had attributed it to some natural caprice of the earth. That is why no one meddled with Elzeard Bouffier's work. If he had been detected he would have had opposition. He was indetectable. Who in the villages or in the administration could have dreamed of such perseverance in a magnificent generosity?

To have anything like a precise idea of his exceptional character one must not forget that he worked in total solitude: so total that, toward the end of his life, he lost the habit of speech. Or perhaps it was that he had no need for it.

In 1933 he received a visit from a forest ranger who notified him of an order against lighting fires out of doors for fear of endangering the growth of this natural forest. It was the first time, the man told him naively, that he had ever heard of a forest growing of its own accord. At that time Bouffier was about to plant beeches at a spot some twelve kilometers from his cottage. In order to avoid travelling back and forth—for he was then seventy-five—he planned to build a stone cabin right at the plantation. The next year he did so.

In 1935 a whole delegation came from the Government to examine the "natural forest." There was a high official from the Forest Service, a deputy, technicians. There was a great deal of ineffectual talk. It was decided that something must be done and, fortunately, nothing was done except the only helpful thing: the whole forest was placed under the protection of the State, and charcoal burning prohibited. For it was impossible not to be captivated by the beauty of those young trees in the fullness of health, and they cast their spell over the deputy himself.

A friend of mine was among the forestry officers of the delegation. To him I explained the mystery. One day the following week we went together to see Elzeard Bouffier. We found him hard at work, some ten kilometers from the spot where the inspection had taken place.

This forester was not my friend for nothing. He was aware of values. He knew how to keep silent. I delivered the eggs I had brought as a present. We shared our lunch among the three of us and spent several hours in wordless contemplation of the countryside.

In the direction from which we had come the slopes were covered with trees twenty to twenty-five feet tall. I remembered how the land had looked in 1913: a desert. . . . Peaceful, regular toil, the vigorous mountain air, frugality and, above all, serenity of spirit had endowed this old man with awe-inspiring health. He was one of God's athletes. I wondered how many more acres he was going to cover with trees.

Before leaving, my friend simply made a brief suggestion about certain species of trees that the soil here seemed particularly suited for. He did not force the point. "For the very good reason," he told me later, "that Bouffier knows more about it than I do." At the end of an hour's walking—having turned it over in his mind—he added, "He knows a lot more about it than anybody. He's discovered a wonderful way to be happy!"

It was thanks to this officer that not only the forest but also the happiness of the man was protected. He delegated three rangers to the task, and so terrorized them that they remained proof against all the bottles of wine the char-coalburners could offer.

The only serious danger to the work occurred during the War of 1939. As cars were being run on gazogenes (wood-burning generators), there was never enough wood. Cutting was started among the oaks of 1910, but the area was so far from any railroads that the enterprise turned out to be financially unsound. It was abandoned. The shepherd had seen nothing of it. He was thirty kilometers away, peacefully continuing his work, ignoring the War of '39 as he had ignored that of '14.

I saw Elzeard Bouffier for the last time in June of 1945. He was then eighty-seven. I had started back along the route through the wastelands; but now, in spite of the disorder in which the war had left the country, there was a bus running between the Durance Valley and the mountain. I attributed the fact that I no longer recognized the scenes of my earlier journeys to this relatively speedy transportation. It seemed to me, too, that the route took me through new territory. It took the name of a village to convince me that I was actually in that region that had been all ruins and desolation.

The bus put me down at Vergons. In 1913, this hamlet of ten or twelve houses had three inhabitants. They had been savage creatures, hating one another, living by trapping game, little removed, both physically and morally, from the conditions of prehistoric man. All about them nettles were feeding upon the remains of abandoned houses. Their condition had been beyond hope. For them, nothing but to await death—a situation which rarely predisposes to virtue.

Everything was changed. Even the air. Instead of the harsh dry winds that used to attack me, a gentle breeze was blowing, laden with scents. A sound like water came from the mountains: it was the wind in the forest. Most amazing of all, I heard the actual sound of water falling into a pool. I saw that a fountain had been built, that it flowed freely and—what touched me most—that someone had planted a linden beside it, a linden that must have been four years old, already in full leaf, the incontestable symbol of resurrection.

Besides, Vergons bore evidence of labor at the sort of undertaking for which hope is required. Hope, then, had returned. Ruins had been cleared away, dilapidated walls torn down and five houses restored. Now there were twenty-eight inhabitants, four of them young married couples. The new houses, freshly plastered, were surrounded by gardens where vegetables and roses, leeks and snapdragons, celery and anemones grew. It was now a village where one would like to live.

From that point on I went on foot. The war just finished had not yet allowed the full blooming of life, but Lazarus was out of the tomb. On the lower slopes of the mountain I saw little fields of barley and of rye; deep in the narrow valleys the meadows were turning green.

It has taken only the eight years since then for the whole

countryside to glow with health and prosperity. On the site of ruins I had seen in 1913 now stand neat farms, cleanly plastered, testifying to a happy and comfortable life. The old streams, fed by the rains and snows that the forest conserves, are flowing again. Their waters have been channeled. On each farm, in groves of maples, fountain pools overflow on to carpets of fresh mint. Little by little the villages have been rebuilt. People from the plains, where land is costly, have settled here, bringing youth, motion, the spirit of adventure. Along the roads you meet hearty men and women, boys and girls who understand laughter and have recovered a taste for picnics. Counting the former population, unrecognizable now that they live in comfort, more than ten thousand people owe their happiness to Elzeard Bouffier.

When I reflect that one man, armed only with his own physical and moral resources, was able to cause this land of Canaan to spring from the wasteland, I am convinced that in spite of everything, humanity is admirable. But when I compute the unfailing greatness of spirit and the tenacity of benevolence that it must have taken to achieve this result, I am taken with an immense respect for that old and unlearned peasant who was able to complete a work worthy of God.

Elzeard Bouffier died peacefully in 1947 at the hospice in Banon.

JOHN STEWART COLLIS

FROM *The Triumph of the Tree*

I have walked in woods so silent and secretive with hidden waiting powers that I have almost felt as if I were in a haunted house. Imagine the effect of untamed forests upon the minds unscored by knowledge. We have all seen stunted ash trees look like witches, we have seen the lichen–hoary wrecks of fallen trunks abandoned to the reign of moss and mounted by strange shapes of fungi take on a fearful aspect. We have seen many a still ghost in the darkness of snowy nights on winter boughs. We have seen mists clinging to the lower world and as frightening in their silence as shades risen from the gloomy pit of deepest Erebus. We have heard voices, echoing through woods and the cries of children raised, though neither man nor child were there. We have lost our way when far from home, while the forbidding boles betrayed us into futile gropings for our goal. When the mind of man was first confronted with these things in a far more fearful form and where his body was anything but safe from harms and his days were ringed and ruled by plans for sheer survival in the midst of many foes, we can understand if only dimly how his fancy ran away with him and he saw a thousand things that were not there.

He heard real sounds and then conjured up their shapes before his eyes. He saw gods and demons—he saw ogres, spirits, genii, and jinns. He saw witches, goblins, and trolls: he saw nymphs and gnomes, naiads and fauns, dryads and hama-dryads—he saw satyrs and centaurs, cyclops and silvani—he saw fairies, elves, brownies, pixies and leprechauns. He peopled the woods with creatures who never existed.

HERMANN HESSE

FROM *Wandering*

For me, trees have always been the most penetrating preachers. I revere them when they live in tribes and families, in forests and groves. And even more I revere them when they stand alone. They are like lonely persons. Not like hermits who have stolen away out of some weakness, but like great, solitary men, like Beethoven and Nietzsche. In their highest boughs the world rustles, their roots rest in infinity; but they do not lose themselves there, they struggle with all the force of their lives for one thing only: to fulfill themselves according to their own laws, to build up their own form, to represent themselves. Nothing is holier, nothing is more exemplary than a beautiful, strong tree. When a tree is cut down and reveals its naked death-wound to the sun, one can read its whole history in the luminous, inscribed disk of its trunk: in the rings of its years, its scars, all the struggle, all the suffering, all the sickness, all the happiness and prosperity stand truly written, the narrow years and the luxurious years, the attacks withstood, the storms endured. And every young farmboy knows that the hardest and noblest wood has the narrowest rings, that high on the mountains and in continuing danger the most indestructible, the strongest, the ideal trees grow.

Trees are sanctuaries. Whoever knows how to speak to them, whoever knows how to listen to them, can learn the truth. They do not preach learning and precepts, they preach, undeterred by particulars, the ancient law of life. A tree says, a kernel is hidden in me, a spark, a thought, I am life from eternal life. The attempt and the risk that the eternal mother took with me is unique, unique the form and veins of my skin, unique the smallest play of leaves in my branches and the smallest scar on my bark. I was made to form and reveal the eternal in my smallest special detail.

A tree says: My strength is trust. I know nothing about my fathers. I know nothing about the thousand children that every year spring out of me. I live out the secret of my seed to the very end, and I care for nothing else. I trust that God is in me. I trust that my labor is holy. Out of this trust I live.

When we are stricken and cannot bear our lives any longer, then a tree has something to say to us: Be still! Be still! Look at me! Life is not easy, life is not difficult. Those are childish thoughts. Let God speak within you, and your thoughts will grow silent. You are anxious because your path leads away from mother and home. But every step and every day lead you back again to the mother. Home is neither here nor there. Home is within you, or home is nowhere at all.

A longing to wander tears my heart when I hear trees rustling in the wind at evening. If one listens to them silently for a long time, this longing reveals its kernel, its meaning. It is not so much a matter of escaping from one's suffering, though it may seem to be so. It is a longing for home, for a memory of the mother, for new metaphors for life. It leads home. Every path leads homeward, every step is birth, every step is death, every grave is mother.

So the tree rustles in the evening, when we stand uneasy before our own childish thoughts. Trees have long thoughts, long-breathing and restful, just as they have longer lives than ours. They are wiser than we are, as long as we do not listen to them. But when we have learned how to listen to trees, then the brevity and the quickness and the childlike hastiness of our thoughts achieve an incomparable joy. Whoever has learned how to listen to trees no longer wants to be a tree. He wants to be nothing except what he is. That is home. That is happiness.

Translated by James Wright

HENRY DAVID THOREAU

Walking

When I would recreate myself, I seek the darkest wood, the thickest and most interminable and, to the citizen, most dismal swamp. I enter a swamp as a sacred place,—a sanctum sanctorum. There is the strength, the marrow of Nature. The wild-wood covers the virgin mould,—and the same soil is good for men and for trees. A man's health requires as many acres of meadow to his prospect as his farm does loads of muck. There are the strong meats on which he feeds. A town is saved, not more by the righteous men in it than by the woods and swamps that surround it. A township where one primitive forest waves above, while another primitive forest rots below,—such a town is fitted to raise not only corn and potatoes, but poets and philosophers for the coming ages. In such a soil grew Homer and Confucius and the rest, and out of such a wilderness comes the Reformer eating locusts and wild honey.

To preserve wild animals implies generally the creation of a forest for them to dwell in or resort to. So is it with man. A hundred years ago they sold bark in our streets peeled from our own woods. In the very aspect of those primitive and rugged trees, there was, methinks, a tanning principle which hardened and consolidated the fibres of men's thoughts. Ah! already I shudder for these comparatively degenerate days of my native village, when you cannot collect a load of bark of good thickness,—and we no longer produce tar and turpentine.

The civilized nations—Greece, Rome, England—have been sustained by the primitive forests which anciently rotted where they stand. They survive as long as the soil is not exhausted. Alas for human culture! little is to be expected of a nation, when the vegetable mould is exhausted and it is compelled to make manure of the bones of its fathers. There the poet sustains himself merely by his own superfluous fat, and the philosopher comes down on his marrow-bones.

ANTON CHEKHOV

FROM *Uncle Vanya*

ASTROFF. No, I won't be able to do that. It will be too late. Now where, where—Look here, my man, get me a glass of vodka, will you? Where—where—One of the characters in Ostroff's plays is a man with a long moustache and short wits, like me. However, let me bid you good-bye, ladies and gentlemen. I should be really delighted if you would come to see me some day with Miss Sonia. My estate is small, but if you are interested in such things I should like to show you a nursery and seedbed whose like you will not find within a thousand miles of here. My place is surrounded by government forests. The forester is old and always ailing, so I superintend almost all the work myself.

HELENA. I have always heard that you were very fond of woods. Of course one can do a great deal of good by helping to preserve them, but does not that work interfere with your real calling?

ASTROFF. God alone knows what a man's real calling is.

HELENA. And do you find it interesting?

ASTROFF. Yes, very.

VOITSKI. Oh, extremely!

HELENA. You are still young, not over thirty-six or seven, I should say, and I suspect that the woods do not interest you as much as you say they do. I should think you would find them monotonous.

S O N I A. No, the work is thrilling. Dr. Astroff watches over the old woods and sets out new plantations every year, and he has already received a diploma and a bronze medal. If you will listen to what he can tell you, you will agree with him entirely. He says that forests are the ornaments of the earth, that they teach mankind to understand beauty and attune his mind to lofty sentiments. Forests temper a stern climate, and in countries where the climate is milder, less strength is wasted in the battle with nature, and the people are kind and gentle. The inhabitants of such countries are handsome, tractable, sensitive, graceful in speech and gesture. Their philosophy is joyous, art and science blossom among them, their treatment of women is full of exquisite nobility—

V O I T S K I. Bravo! Bravo! All that is very pretty, but it is also unconvincing. So, my friend you must let me go on burning firewood in my stoves and building my sheds of planks.

A S T R O F F. You can burn peat in your stoves and build your sheds of stone. Oh, I don't object, of course, to cutting wood from necessity, but why destroy the forests! The woods of Russia are trembling under the blows of the axe. Millions of trees have perished. The homes of the wild animals and birds have been desolated; the rivers are shrinking, and many beautiful landscapes are gone for ever. And why? Because men are too lazy and stupid to stoop down and pick up their fuel from the ground. Am I not right, Madame? Who but a stupid barbarian could burn so much beauty in his stove and destroy that which he cannot make? Man is endowed with reason and the power to create, so that he may increase that which has been given him, but until now he has not created, but demolished. The forests are disappearing, the rivers are running dry, the game is exterminated, the climate is spoiled, and the earth becomes poorer and uglier every day. I read irony in your eye;

you do not take what I am saying seriously, and—and—after all, it may very well be nonsense. But when I pass peasant-forests that I have preserved from the axe, or hear the rustling of the young plantations set out with my own hands, I feel as if I had some small share in improving the climate, and that if mankind is happy a thousand years from now I will have been a little bit responsible for their happiness. When I plant a little birch tree and then see it budding into young green and sway-ing in the wind, my heart swells with pride and I—however—I must be off. Probably it is all nonsense, anyway. Good-bye.

Translated by Marian Fell

PIERRE DE RONSARD

Against the Woodcutter of the Forest of Gastine

Hold a while, woodman, stay your arm and hear:
This is not wood which you cast proudly down;
Do you not see the blood which spurts and streams,
The blood of nymphs who lived within that bark?

Impious murderer, if hanging is the price
Of those who pilfer things of little worth,
How many fires and chains, deaths, miseries,
Should be your due, who killed our goddesses?

High forest, woodland mansion of the birds!
Never again shall harts or lonely deer

Pasture your shadowed glades, and your green lawns
Never again receive the summer sunlight.

Never again shall lovelorn shepherd sit
Against some tree, tuning his flageolet,
His hound stretched at his feet, and crook at side,
To tell his love for beautiful Jeannette:
All will be mute; Echo will have no voice;
You will be meadows, and where your trees were once,
Whose dim seen shadows slowly shift and stir,
You will feel the cutting plough and coulter sharp;
Your silence lost, Pan and his Satyrs fled,
No more the deer shall hide his fauns in you.

Farewell, old forest, Zephyr's favoured plaything,
Where first I learned to tune my lyre's tongues;
Where first I heard the arrows echoing
Of Bright Apollo, and wondered in my heart;
Where first I wooed Calliope the fair,
And fell in love with all her poetry,
When on my brow she threw a hundred roses,
And Euterpe herself gave me her milk.

Farewell, old forest, farewell sacred heads,
At all times high revered by field and flowers,
And now the scorn of all the passers-by
Who, burning in summer from the airy rays,
No longer find the cool green of your shade:
Let these indict your murderers, and revile them!

Farewell, oaks, fair crown of bravest hillsides,
Jupiter's trees, and sprung from old Dodona,
Who first gave men a tree for their delight:

Pierre de Ronsard

Ungrateful men, who have not recognised
The rich they had of you—a monstrous people
To slaughter so those who had cherished them!

Oh hapless man that trusteth in the world!
You gods, how true is that philosophy,
Which says that all things perish in the end
And, changing from one form, assume another!

Some day Tempe's vale will be a hill,
Mount Athos' peak will be an open plain;
Neptune some time will wave with growing corn:
Matter endures though form be lost for ever.

Translated by William Stirling

JEAN DE LA FONTAINE

The Woods and the Woodman

A certain wood-chopper lost or broke
From his axe's eye a bit of oak.
The forest must needs be somewhat spared
While such a loss was being repaired.
Came the man at last, and humbly prayed,
That the woods would kindly lend to him—
A moderate loan—a single limb,
Whereof might another helve be made,
And his axe should elsewhere drive its trade
Oh the oaks and firs that then might stand,
For their ancientness and glorious charms!
The innocent Forest lent him arms;
But bitter indeed was her regret,
For the wretch, his axe new helved and whet,
Did nought but his benefactress spoil
Of the finest trees, that graced her soil,
And ceaselessly was she made to groan,
Doing penance for that fatal loan.

Behold the world-stage and its actors,
Where benefits hurt benefactors!
A weary theme and full of pain;
For where's the shade so cool and sweet
Protecting strangers from the heat,

But of such a wrong complain?
Alas! I vex myself in vain;
Ingratitude, do what I will,
Is sure to be the fashion still.

JOHN STEWART COLLIS

Farewell to the Wood

In the company of flowers we know happiness. In the company of trees we are able to "think"—they foster meditation. Trees are very intellectual. There is nowhere on earth we can think so well as in a thin wood resting against a tree. Such at least is my experience and it is the ultimate memory that I shall carry away from this place. For in parting I know that the greatest wrench of all is in connection with the old oak tree (under which I have written this account). It is not easy to say farewell to it.

WAKAYAMA BOKUSUI

Trees

Do people really know that stillness which grows out of the tree-covered earth? In particular the stillness of such enormous, old tree statures which do not know anything of time and stand there over epochs away. When I think of the most various phenomenon of the world of nature, I always feel silence. I am overcome by the yearning of peace. But I feel it most intimately when I observe trees. Or when I look at the forest and think of it. In the silence of trees, there is a certain brightness. There is warmth. The forest, however, throws some cooler shadows. All the more, the stillness deepens. Softly, very softly, the echo of the various voices of birds penetrates into my ear.

WANG WEI

Light Lives on My Wang River Retreat

Willow branches sweeping the ground—
    not worth cutting
Pine trees touching the clouds
    and growing further still
Wisteria soon giving darkness
    for monkeys to hide in
Oak leaves so abundant
    I might keep musk deer

IVAN TURGENEV

A Tour in the Forest

The sight of the vast, pine wood embracing the whole horizon—the sight of the "Forest" recalls the sight of the ocean and the sensation it arouses are the same—the same primeval untouched force lies outstretched in its breadth and majesty, before the eyes of the spectator. From the heart of the eternal forest, from the undying bosom of the waters comes the same voice—"I have nothing to do with thee" nature says to man. "I reign supreme while do thou bestir thyself to thy utmost to escape dying." But the forest is gloomier and more monotonous than the sea, especially the pine forest which is always alike and almost soundless. . . . The ocean menaces and caresses, it frolics with every color, speaks with every voice— it reflects the sky from which too comes the breath of eternity, but an eternity as it were not so remote from us. The dark unchanging pine forest keeps sullen silence or is filled with a dull roar and at the sight of it sinks into man's heart more deeply, more irresistibly the sense of his own nothingness. It is hard for man, the creature of a day, born yesterday and doomed to death on the morrow. It is hard for him to bare the cold gaze of the eternal Isis, fixed without sympathy upon him. Not only the daring hopes and dreams are humbled and quenched within him, enfolded by the icy breath of the elements—no, his whole soul sinks down and swoons within him—he feels that the last of his kind may vanish off the face of the earth and not one needle will quiver on those twigs. He feels his isolation, his feebleness, his fortuitousness—and in hurried secret panic he turns to the petty cares and labors of life—he is more at ease in that world he has himself created—there he is at home; there he dares, yet believes in his own importance and in his own power.

Translated by Constance Garnett

JOHN FOWLES

FROM *The Tree*

Perhaps because I was brought up without any orthodox faith and remain without it, there was also I suspect some religious element in my feelings towards woods. Their mysterious atmospheres, their silences, the parallels, especially in beechwoods—with columned naves, that Baudelaire seized on in his famous line about a temple of living pillars—all these must recall the man-made holy place. We know that the very first places in Neolithic times, long before Stonehenge (which is only a petrified copse), were artificial wooden groves, make of felled, transported and re-erected tree trunks and that their roof must have seemed to their makers less roofs than artificial canopies. Even the smallest woods have their secrets and secret places, their unmarked precincts and I am certain all sacred buildings from the greatest cathedral to the smallest chapel and in all religions derive from the natural aura of certain woodland or forest settings. In them we stand among older, larger and infinitely other beings remoter from us than the most bizarre other non-human forms of life—blind, immobile, speechless (on speaking only Baudelaire "confuses paroles") waiting, altogether very like the only form a universal god could conceivably take. The Neolithic peoples, the slaves as we are of an industrial economy of their own great new culture, of their own great new cultural 'invention' of farming were the first great deforesters of our landscapes and perhaps it was guilt that made them return to the trees to find a model for their religious buildings—in which they were followed by the Bronze Age, the Greeks and Romans with their columns and porticoes, the Celtic Iron Age with its Druids and sacred oak groves. . . .

There was certainly something erotic in these as there is in all places that isolate and hide but woods in any case are highly sensuous things. They may not carry more species than some other environments but they are far richer and more dramatic in sensory impressions. Nowhere are the two great contemporary modes of reproducing reality, the word and the camera more at a loss, less able to capture the sound (or soundlessness) and the scents, the temperatures and moods, the all foundness, the different levels of being in the vertical ascent, from ground to tree top, in the variety of different beings themselves and the subtlety of their inter-relationships. In a way woods are like the sea, sensorily far too various and immense for anything but surfaces or glimpses to be captured—they defeat viewfinder, drawing paper, canvas. They cannot be framed and words are as futile, hopelessly too laborious and used to capture the reality. . . .

It is not for nothing that the ancestors of the modern novel that began to appear in the early Middle Ages so frequently had the forest for setting and the quest for central theme. Never mind that the actual forest often is a monotonous thing—the metaphorical forest is constant suspense stage awaiting actors, heroes, maidens, dragons, mysterious castles at every step.

It may be useless as a literal setting in an age that has lost all belief in maidens, dragons and magical castles, but I think we have only superficially abandoned the basic recipe (danger, eroticism, search) first discovered by those early medieval writers. We have simply transferred the tree setting to the now more familiar brick and concrete forest of town and city. Older and less planned quarters of cities and towns are profoundly woodlike and especially in this matter of the mode of their passage through us, the way they unreel, disorientate, open-close, surprise, please. The stupidest mistake of all the many stupid mistakes of twentieth century architecture has been to forget this ancient model in the more grandiose town planning. Geometric, linear cities make geometric, linear people. Wood cities make human beings. . . .

There is a spiritual corollary to the way we are currently deforesting and denaturing our planet. In the end what we must most defoliate and deprive is ourselves. . . .

The threat to us in the coming millennium lies not in nature seen as a rogue shark, but in our growing emotional and intellectual detachment from it, and I do not think the remedy lies solely in the success or failure of the conservation movement. It lies as much in our admitting the debit side of the scientific revolution and especially the changes it has affected in our modes of perceiving and of experiencing the world as individuals. Unlike white sharks, trees do not even possess the ability to defend themselves. What arms they sometimes have like thorns are static, and their size and immobility means they cannot hide. They are the most defenseless of creation in regard to man, universally placed by him below the level of animate feeling and so the most prone to destruction. Their main evolutionary defense, as with many social animals, birds and fishes, lies in their innumerability, that is, their capacity to reproduce in which for trees longevity plays a major part. Perhaps it is this passive patient nature of their system of self preservation that has allowed man, despite his ancient fears of what they may harbor in terms of other creatures and the supernatural, to forgive them in one aspect—to see something that is also protective, maternal, even womb-like in their silent depths.

All through history trees have provided sanctuary and refuge for both the justly and the unjustly persecuted and hunted. There are freedoms in woods that our ancestors perhaps realized more fully than we do—a retreat from the normal world. In the long cultivated and economically exploited lands of the world, our woodlands are the last fragments of comparatively unadultered nature and so the most accessible outward correlatives and providers of the relationship, the feeling, the knowledge that we are in danger of losing—the last green churches and chapels outside the walled civilization and culture we have made without tools.

The return to the green chaos, the deep forest and refuge of the unconscious is a nightly phenomenon and one that psychiatrists—and torturers—tell us is essential to the human mind. Without it, it disintegrates and goes mad. If I cherish trees beyond all personal (and perhaps rather peculiar) need and liking of them, it is because of this, their natural correspondence with the greener, more mysterious processes of mind—and because they also seem to me the best, most revealing messengers to us from all nature, the nearest its heart.

THOMAS JEFFERSON

To Martha Jefferson Randolph—1793

I never before knew the full value of trees. My house is entirely embosomed in high plane trees with good grass below and under them I breakfast, dine, write, read and receive my company. What would I not give that the trees planted nearest round the house at Monticello were full grown.

MADAME DE SÉVIGNÉ

Les Rochers

(*Sunday, 27 October 1675*)

I am glad to be home and am making a new alley which fills my leisure hours. . . . and after all my dear—life goes so quickly and so soon must we reach our appointed end, that it is often a matter of surprise to me that we can suffer such profound dejection from purely mundane considerations. I have plenty of time for reflection and if my woods fail to inspire me, I have only myself to blame.

FRANÇOIS RENÉ DE CHATEAUBRIAND

I am deeply attached to my trees. I address to them elegies and sonnets and odes. I know them all by their names like my children. They are my family. I have no other and I hope to die in the midst of them.

JOHN STEWART COLLIS

FROM *The Worm Forgives the Plough*

Truly trees are Beings. We feel that to be so. Hence their silence, their indifference to us is almost exasperating. We would speak to them, we would ask their message—for they seem to hold some weighty truth, some special secret.

And of all the phenomena concerning trees, that which appeals to me most is the trunk. For me the most beautiful sight in the woods is not the foliage, not the flowers, not the squirrel, not the deer—it is the trunk of trees of about thirty years upward. Especially the ash (of all trees ash becomes fire best)—the smooth grey bark, then a patch of dark moss, above it a patch of pale green lichen in beautiful filigree pressed against the bark, then a number of white spots, then bark again, then moss again. No pattern, yet all pattern, no design, yet all design, making a rounded tapestry beyond all the powers of art to render. No bright colors, yet many colors, and in winter time how often we see from the train window tree trunks almost as green as green set in the gloom of the leafless boughs, taking the rain and the dusk in silent alertness—often I have been glad that I am not a painter never more so than when confronted by some magnificent tree trunk. Here is something that cannot be told, cannot be rendered. Here is the object, the thing itself so staggering in its presence that we fall back from it, the intricacy of the totality cannot be copied, and it is the intricacy that is the picture . . . Look at that old silver birch trunk. Knuckled, knotched and dented with its ditches, ruts and causeways—all subservient to the majority of the design—look at the splashes of smooth white irregularly placed—the bark itself—no lichen—if a house painter did a post with dabs of white here and there, we would think it a poor strange piece of work—but here it is magnificent, the impression of the whole terrific. We must leave our pen and brush in place of it—abandon art as a hopeless substitute— look at that old scotch pine. It has no lichen—all the beauty is in the bark alone—rubbed, fluted, seamed, deeply chiselled— it is a personality, it is a Being. Perhaps that's what I'm after here in these fumbling words—the power and the glory here is in the "substance" of the thing and art is without substance. . . .

RALPH WALDO EMERSON

FROM *Nature*

In the woods, too, a man casts off his years as the snake his slough and what period soever of life is always a child. In the woods is perpetual youth. Within these plantations of God, a decorum and sanctity reign, a perennial festival is dressed and the guest sees not how he should tire of them in a thousand years. In the woods we return to reason and faith. There I feel that nothing can befall me in life—no disgrace, no calamity (leaving me my eyes) which nature cannot repair. Standing on the bare ground—my head bathed by the blithe air and uplifted into infinite space—all mean egotism vanishes. I become a transparent eyeball. I am nothing. I see all: the currents of the Universal Being circulate through me; I am part or parcel of God. The name of the nearest friend sounds then foreign and accidental: to be brothers, to be acquaintances, master or servant, is then a trifle and a disturbance. I am the lover of uncontained and immortal beauty. In the wilderness I find something more dear and connate than in streets or villages. In the tranquil landscape and especially in the distant line of the horizon man beholds somewhat as beautiful as his own nature. The greatest delight which the fields and woods minister is the suggestion of an occult relation between man and the vegetable. I am not alone and unacknowledged. They nod to me and I to them. The waving of the boughs in the storms is new to me and old. It takes me by surprise, and yet is not unknown. Its effect is like that of a higher thought or a better emotion coming over me when I deemed I was thinking justly or doing right.

ANTHONY RYE

Sea Trees

Mark these low-trees, the sculptural winds have
  moulded
These old, gale-bitten, crouched and cowering trees!
No bough of each but to the storms has yielded
No harassed bough's last leaf: they never cease
To bear them to the shore tormentedly;
    Even in the attitude to fly
The surging seas, the salt, corrosive spray.

      .   .   .

But mark these trees: terror of tempest forms them
And yet, compact of courage, stubborn, hale
Through bitterness of flight how well they know
What fittest arms them;
And they endure, close in their shaggy mail
All frayed grey shoots, gaunt roots, and they are slow
To fail, fear makes them brave
To stand and fight till the last storm's last wave.

EUGÈNE DELACROIX

FROM *Journal of Eugène Delacroix*

(*Monday, May 9th*)

Noticing the Antin Oak from a distance, I did not recognize it at first, finding it so ordinary. . . . At the distance necessary for the eye to seize it as a whole, it seems to be of ordinary size: if I place myself under its branches the impression changes completely: perceiving only the trunk which I almost touch and the springing-point of the thick branches which spread out over my head like the immense arms of the giant of the forest. I am astonished at the grandeur of its details. . . . In a word I see it as big, and even terrifying in its bigness. When I get under the branches themselves and see only parts, unrelated to the ensemble, I experience the sensation of the sublime. I have often said that the branches of the tree were themselves small complete trees.

Translated by Walter Pack

ANTOINE DE SAINT-EXUPÉRY

FROM *Terre des Hommes*

One evening we had dined at the fort and the commandant had shown off his garden to us. Someone had sent him from France, three thousand miles away, a few boxes of real soil and out of this soil grew three green leaves which we caressed as if they had been jewels. The commandant would say of them "This is my park." And when there arose one of those sand storms that shrivelled everything up, he would move the park down into the cellar.

Translated by Lewis Galantiere

ANTOINE DE SAINT-EXUPÉRY

FROM *Wind, Sand & Stars*

I stopped to waken a sleeping Bedouin and he turned into the trunk of a black tree. A tree trunk? Here in the desert? I was amazed and bent over to lift a broken bough. It was solid marble.

Straightening up I looked around and saw more black marble. An antediluvian forest littered the ground with its broken tree tops. How many thousand years ago under what hurricane of the time of Genesis, had this cathedral of wood crumbled in this spot? Countless centuries had rolled these fragments of giant pillars at my feet, polished them like steel and petrified and vitrified them and imbued them with the color of jet.

I could distinguish the knots in their branches, the twistings of their once living boughs, could count the rings of life in them. This forest had rustled with birds and been filled with music that now was struck by doom and frozen into salt.

Translated by Lewis Galantiere

JOHN STEWART COLLIS

FROM *The Triumph of the Tree*

Trees promote meditation. Their silence is almost like unspoken thoughts. They are indeed the friends of philosophers. We enter the wood. We leave behind the world that is too much with us—it has wholly gone. We tread the silent glades in silence. Here is the reign of peace. Here the mind is suddenly purified. See that noble old oak. There is a place for meditation. Beneath those shady boughs in the stillness of that room, shall we not come to truth? Could we sit long enough, we feel, in this unsurpassed calm, and balk the screaming duties that are not real within these gates and flaunt the clock we call time—then we too would be enlightened.

ROBERT WALSER

FROM *The Walk*

I came into a pine forest, through which coiled a smiling, serpentine, and at the same time roguishly graceful path, which I followed with pleasure. Path and forest floor were as a carpet, and here within the forest it was quiet as in a happy human soul, as in the interior of a temple, as in a palace and enchanted dream-wrapped fairy-tale castle, as in Sleeping Beauty's castle, where all sleep, and all are hushed for centuries of long years. I penetrated deeper, and I speak perhaps a little indulgently if I say that to myself I seemed like a prince with golden hair, his body clad in warrior's armor. So solemn was it in the forest that lovely and solemn imaginings, quite of their own accord, took possession of the sensitive walker there. How glad I was at this sweet forest softness and repose! From time to time, from outside, a slight sound or two penetrated the delicious seclusion and bewitching darkness, perhaps a bang, a whistle, or some other noise, whose distant note would only intensify the prevailing soundlessness, which I inhaled to my very heart's content, and whose virtues I drank and quaffed with due ceremony. Here and there in all this tranquillity and quietude a bird let his blithe voice be heard out of his charmed and holy hiding place. Thus I stood and listened, and suddenly there came upon me an inexpressible feeling for the world, and, together with it, a feeling of gratitude, which broke powerfully out of my soul. The pines stood straight as pillars there, and not the least thing moved in the whole delicate forest, throughout which all kinds of inaudible voices seemed to echo and sound. Music out of the primeval world, from whence I cannot tell, stole on my ear. "Oh, thus, if it must be, shall I then willingly end and die. A memory will then delight me even in the grave, and a gratitude enliven me even in death; a thanksgiving for the pleasures, for the joys, for the ecstasies; a thanksgiving for life, and a joy at joy." High up, a gentle rustling, whispering down from the treetops, could be heard. "To love and to kiss here must be divinely beautiful," I told myself. Simply to tread on the pleasant ground became a joy, and the stillness kindled prayers in the feeling soul. "To be dead here, and to lie inconspicuous in the cool forest earth must be sweet. Oh, that one could sense and enjoy death even in death! Perhaps one can. To have a small, quiet grave in the forest would be lovely. Perhaps I should hear the singing of the birds and the forest rustling above me. I would like that." Marvelous between trunks of oaks a pillar of sunbeams fell into the forest, which to me seemed like a delicious green grave. Soon I stepped out into the radiant open again, and into life.

Translated by Christopher Middleton

ROSA BONHEUR

These are the trees to which Denecourt was kind enough to give my name, she said. See how those leaves have become luminous in the last rays of the sun. Have they not the transparency of the most magnificent stained glass windows? No, there are none more splendid in any basilica. It was forests of tall trees like this one with its intertwining branches that gave the architects of the Middle Ages the inspiration for their cathedral vaults. The leaves that fall in the autumn, the sap that rises in the spring—is that not, after all, the symbol of the life to come? The temples of the Druids were their forests. That is where mine is too, and that is where I go to pray to God and to thank him for the blessings he has showered on me throughout my career.

PIERRE-JAKEZ HÉLIAS

FROM *Le Cheval d'Orgueil*

Nothing is more beautiful than a tree, Alain Le Goff likes to say. The poor man does not possess a single tree of his own, but all those that he can see with his eyes are his partners in Creation's great game. There are some that he likes better than others. These are not the most triumphant, but the ones that struggle to survive in the fierce wind. He goes to see them in the winter, when they are naked.

"Look how they are working," he says. "And what are they doing, Grandfather?" "They're connecting the earth to the sky. It's very difficult, my boy. The sky is so light that it's always on the point of taking flight. If there were no trees, it would bid us goodbye. And then there would be nothing left for us but to die. God forbid!" "But there are some countries where not a single tree grows. I learned that at school. They're called deserts." "That's just it, my boy. There are no men in those parts. The sky has taken off."

I pretend not to understand. He lights his pipe, smiling. No one has ever smiled like Alain Le Goff, and that's why men are unhappy on earth. He slaps the gnarled trunk with his open hand: "You can see quite clearly that a tree trunk is a big rope. It even has knots in it, sometimes. The strands of the rope work loose at either end, so as to fasten on to the sky and the earth. They are called branches up above, and roots down below. But it's the same thing. The roots try to find their way in the earth in the same manner as the branches work their way into the sky." "But it's more difficult to get into the earth than into the sky." "Not at all! If that were true, the branches would be straight. But just look how twisted they are on this apple tree! They have to try to find their way, I tell you. They grow, the sky resists, and they change direction as often as is necessary. They have a lot of trouble, you know. Perhaps even more trouble than the roots down below." "And what is it that gives them so much trouble, Grandfather?" "It's the wind, the putrid wind. The wind would like to separate the sky from the earth. It thrusts its tongue between them. And behind it, the sea is waiting to come and cover everything over. But the trees hold out at both ends. The blessed sun comes to the aid of the branches, while the rain refreshes the roots. It's a tremendous battle, my boy. Things never stop battling, in this world." "What about us, then? What must we do?" "Have confidence in the trees against the wind."

Translated by June Guicharnaud

ROBERT GIBBINGS

FROM *Lovely Is the Lee*

Listen. Listen again. Tune your being to the song of streams. Close beside a fir tree three sheep are grazing. Stand by the tree and think yourself into it. Touch it with the tips of your fingers. Lay the palms of your hands on its rough bark and feel the tremor of its fibres. Stretch up your spirit towards its topmost branches following each changing urge of growth. Sense its growth, for growth is immortality. We are all but cells, forming and reforming in the elemental tissue, momentary manifestations, glimpses in the microscopes of God. What does the chlorophyll cell in the blade of grass know of biology? Just as much perhaps as we do of eternity.

GEOFFREY CHAUCER

But Lord, so I was glad and well begoon
For over al, where I myn eyen caste
Weren trees, claad with levys that ay
                shall laste
Eche in his kynde with colors fresh and grene

As emeraude, that joy was for the sene
The Bylder oadk and eke the hardy ashe
The pillar elme, the cofre unto careyne
The box pipe tree, holme to whippes
                lasshe
The sayling tirre, the cipress
                   doth to pleyne
The shooter ewe, the aspe for shafters
                pleyne
The olive of pes and eke the drunken vyne
The victor palme, the laurers to
                devyne

AI QUING

Spring 1940

One tree another tree
Each standing alone and erect
The wind and air
Tell their distance apart
But beneath the cover of earth
Their roots reach out
And at depths that cannot be seen
The roots of the trees intertwine.

SELMA LAGERLÖF

The Flight into Egypt

Far away in one of the Eastern deserts many, many years ago grew a palm tree, which was both exceedingly old and exceedingly tall.

All who passed through the desert had to stop and gaze at it, for it was much larger than other palms; and they used to say of it, that someday it would certainly be taller than the obelisks and pyramids.

Where the huge palm tree stood in its solitude and looked out over the desert, it saw something one day which made its mighty leafcrown sway back and forth on its slender trunk with astonishment. Over by the desert borders walked two human beings. They were still at the distance at which camels appear to be as tiny as moths; but they were certainly two human beings—two who were strangers in the desert; for the palm knew the desert-folk. They were a man and a woman who had neither guide nor pack-camels; neither tent nor water-sack.

"Verily," said the palm to itself, "These two have come hither only to meet certain death."

The palm cast a quick, apprehensive glance around.

"It surprises me," it said, "that the lions are not already out to hunt this prey, but I do not see a single one astir; nor do I see any of the desert robbers, but they'll probably soon come."

"A seven-fold death awaits these travellers," thought the palm. "The lions will devour them, thirst will parch them, the sand-storm will bury them, robbers will trap them, sunstroke will blight them, and fear will destroy them—" and the palm tried to think of something else. The fate of these people made it sad at heart.

But on the whole desert plain, which lay spread out beneath the palm, there was nothing which it had not known and looked upon these thousand years. Nothing in particular could arrest its attention. Again it had to think of the two wanderers.

"By the drought and the storm!" said the palm, calling upon Life's most dangerous enemies. "What is that that the woman carries on her arm? I believe these fools also bring a little child with them!"

The palm, who was far-sighted—as the old usually are—actually saw aright. The woman bore on her arm a child, that leaned against her shoulder and slept.

"The child hasn't even sufficient clothing on," said the palm. "I see that the mother has tucked up her skirt and thrown it over the child. She must have snatched him from his bed in great haste and rushed off with him. I understand now: these people are runaways.

"But they are fools, nevertheless," continued the palm. "Unless an angel protects them, they would have done better to have let their enemies do their worst, than to venture into this wilderness.

"I can imagine how the whole thing came about. The man stood at his work; the child slept in his crib; the woman had gone out to fetch water. When she was a few steps from the door, she saw enemies coming. She rushed back to the house, snatched up her child, and fled.

"Since then, they have been fleeing for several days. It is very certain that they have not rested a moment. Yes, everything has happened in this way, but still I say unless an angel protects them—

"They are so frightened that, as yet, they feel neither fatigue nor suffering. But I see their thirst by the strange gleam in their eyes. Surely I ought to know a thirsty person's face!"

And when the palm began to think of thirst, a shudder passed through its tall trunk, and the long leaves' numberless lobes rolled up, as though they had been held over a fire.

"Were I a human being," it said, "I should never venture into the desert. He is pretty brave who dares come here without having roots that reach down to the never-dying water veins. Here it can be dangerous even for palms; yes, even for a palm such as I.

"If I could counsel them, I should beg them to turn back. Their enemies could never be as cruel toward them as the desert. Perhaps they think it is easy to live in the desert! But I know that now and then, even I have found it hard to keep alive. I recollect one time in my youth when a hurricane threw a whole mountain of sand over me. I came near choking. If I could have died that would have been my last moment."

The palm continued to think aloud, as the aged and solitary habitually do.

"I hear a wondrously beautiful melody rush through my leaves," it said. "All the lobes on my leaves are quivering. I know not what it is that takes possession of me at the sight of these poor strangers. But this unfortunate woman is so beautiful! She carries me back, in memory, to the most wonderful thing that I ever experienced."

And while the leaves continued to move in a soft melody, the palm was reminded how once, very long ago, two illustrious personages had visited the oasis. They were the Queen of Sheba and Solomon the Wise. The beautiful Queen was to return to her own country, the King had accompanied her on the journey, and now they were going to part. "In remembrance of this hour," said the Queen then, "I now plant a date seed in the earth, and I wish that from it shall spring a palm which shall grow and live until a King shall arise in Judaea, greater than Solomon." And when she had said this, she planted the seed in the earth and watered it with her tears.

"How does it happen that I am thinking of this just today?" said the palm. "Can this woman be so beautiful that she reminds me of the most glorious of queens, of her by whose word I have lived and flourished until this day?

"I hear my leaves rustle louder and louder," said the palm, "and it sounds as melancholy as a dirge. It is as though they prophesied that some one would soon leave this life. It is well to know that it does not apply to me, since I cannot die."

The palm assumed that the death-rustle in its leaves must apply to the two lone wanderers. It is certain that they too believed that their last hour was nearing. One saw it from their expression as they walked past the skeleton of a camel which lay in their path. One saw it from the glances they cast back at a pair of passing vultures. It couldn't be otherwise; they must perish!

They had caught sight of the palm and oasis and hastened thither to find water. But when they arrived at last, they collapsed from despair, for the well was dry. The woman, worn out, laid the child down and seated herself beside the well-curb, and wept. The man flung himself down beside her and beat upon the dry earth with his fists. The palm heard how they talked with each other about their inevitable death. It also gleaned from their conversation that King Herod had ordered the slaughter of all male children from two to three years old, because he feared that the long-looked-for King of the Jews had been born.

"It rustles louder and louder in my leaves," said the palm. "These poor fugitives will soon see their last moment."

It perceived also that they dreaded the desert. The man said it would have been better if they had stayed at home and fought with the soldiers, than to fly hither. He said that they would have met an easier death.

"God will help us," said the woman.

"We have no food and no water. How should God be able to help us?" In despair he rent his garments and pressed his face against the dry earth. He was without hope—like a man with a death-wound in his heart.

The woman sat erect with her hands clasped over her knees. But the looks she cast toward the desert spoke of a hopelessness beyond bounds.

The palm heard the melancholy rustle in its leaves growing louder and louder. The woman must have heard it also, for she turned her gaze upward toward the palm-crowns. And instantly she involuntarily raised her arms.

"Oh, dates, dates!" she cried. There was such intense

agony in her voice that the old palm wished itself no taller than a broom and that the dates were as easy to reach as the buds on a briar bush. It probably knew that its crown was full of date clusters, but how should a human being reach such a height?

The man had already seen how beyond all reach the date clusters hung. He did not even raise his head. He begged his wife not to long for the impossible.

But the child, who had toddled about by himself and played with sticks and straws, had heard the mother's outcry.

Of course the little one could not imagine that his mother should not get everything she wished for. The instant she said dates, he began to stare at the tree. He pondered and pondered how he should bring down the dates. His forehead was almost drawn into wrinkles under the golden curls. At last a smile stole over his face. He had found the way. He went up to the palm and stroked it with his little hand, and said, in a sweet childish voice:

"Palm, bend thyself! Palm, bend thyself!"

But what was that, what was that? The palm leaves rustled as if a hurricane had passed through them, and up and down the long trunk travelled shudder upon shudder. And the tree felt that the little one was its superior. It could not resist him.

And it bowed its long trunk before the child, as people bow before princes. In a great bow it bent itself toward the ground, and finally it came down so far that the big crown with the trembling leaves swept the desert sand.

The child appeared to be neither frightened nor surprised; with a joyous cry he loosened cluster after cluster from the old palm's crown. When he had plucked enough dates, and the tree still lay on the ground, the child came back again and caressed it and said, in the gentlest voice:

"Palm, raise thyself! Palm, raise thyself!"

Slowly and reverently the big tree raised itself on its slender trunk, while the leaves played like harps.

"Now I know for whom they are playing the death melody," said the palm to itself when it stood erect once more. "It is not for any of these people."

The man and the woman sank upon their knees and thanked God.

"Thou has seen our agony and removed it. Thou art the Powerful One who bendest the palm-trunk like a reed. What enemy should we fear when Thy strength protects us?"

The next time a caravan passed through the desert, the travellers saw that the great palm's leafcrown had withered.

"How can this be?" said a traveller. "This palm was not to die before it had seen a King greater than Solomon."

"Mayhap it has seen him," answered another of the desert travellers.

WALT WHITMAN

I saw in Louisiana a live-oak growing,
All alone stood it and the moss hung down from the branches,
Without any companion it grew there uttering joyous leaves of
    dark green,
And its look, rude, unbending, lusty, made me think of my-
    self,
But I wonder'd how it could utter joyous leaves standing alone
    there without its friend near, for I knew I could not,
And I broke off a twig with a certain number of leaves upon it,
    and twined around it a little moss,
And brought it away, and I have placed it in sight in my room,
It is not needed to remind me as of my own dear friends,
(For I believe lately I think of little else than of them,)
Yet it remains to me a curious token, it makes me think of
    manly love;
For all that, and though the live-oak glistens there in Louisiana
    solitary in a wide flat space,
Uttering joyous leaves all its life without a friend a lover near,
I know very well I could not.

JEAN DE LA FONTAINE

The Oak and the Reed

One day the oak said to the reed:
'You have good cause indeed
To accuse Nature of being unkind.
To you a wren must seem
An intolerable burden, and the least puff of wind
That chances to wrinkle the face of the stream
Forces your head low; whereas I,
Huge as a Caucasian peak, defy
Not only the sun's glare, but the worst the weather can do.
What seems a breeze to me is a gale for you.
Had you been born in the lee of my leaf-sheltered ground,
You would have suffered less, I should have kept you warm;
But you reeds are usually found
On the moist borders of the kingdom of the storm.
It strikes me that to you Nature has been unfair.'

TREES

'Your pity,' the plant replied, 'springs from a kind heart.
But please don't be anxious on my part.
Your fear of the winds ought to be greater than mine.
I bend, but I never break. You, till now, have been able to bear
Their fearful buffets without flexing your spine.
But let us wait and see.' Even as he spoke,
From the horizon's nethermost bloom
The worst storm the north had ever bred in its womb
  Furiously awoke.
The tree stood firm, the reed began to bend.
The wind redoubled its efforts to blow—
  So much so
  That in the end
It uprooted the one that had touched the sky with its head,
But whose feet reached to the region of the dead.

Translated by James Michie

HENRY DAVID THOREAU

Death of a Pine Tree

This afternoon, being on Fair Haven Hill, I heard the sound of a saw, and soon after from the Cliff saw two men sawing down a noble pine beneath, about forty rods off. I resolved to watch it till it fell, the last of a dozen or more which were left when the forest was cut and for fifteen years have waved in solitary majesty over the sprout-land. I saw them like beavers or insects gnawing at the trunk of this noble tree, the diminutive manikins with their cross-cut saw which could scarcely span it. It towered up a hundred feet as I afterward found by measurement, one of the tallest probably in the township and straight as an arrow, but slanting a little toward the hillside, its top seen against the frozen river and the hills of Conantum. I watch closely to see when it begins to move. Now the sawers stop, and with an axe open it a little on the side toward which it leans, that it may break the faster. And now their saw goes again. Now surely it is going; it is inclined one quarter of the quadrant, and, breathless, I expect its crashing fall. But no, I was mistaken; it has not moved an inch; it stands at the same angle as at first. It is fifteen minutes yet to its fall. Still its branches wave in the wind, as if it were destined to stand for a century, and the wind soughs through its needles as of yore; it is still a forest tree, the most majestic tree that waves over Musketaquid. The silvery sheen of the sunlight is reflected from its needles; it still affords an inaccessible crotch for the squirrel's nest; not a lichen has forsaken its mast-like stem, its raking mast,—the hill is the hulk. Now, now's the moment! The manikins at its base are fleeing from their crime. They have dropped the guilty saw and axe. How slowly and majestically it starts! as if it were only swayed by a summer breeze, and would return without a sigh to its location in the air. And now it fans the hillside with its fall, and it lies down to its bed in the valley, from which it is never to rise, as softly as a feather, folding its green mantle about it like a warrior, as if, tired from standing, it embraced the earth with silent joy, returning its elements to the dust again. But hark! there you only saw, but did not hear. There now comes up a deafening crash to these rocks, advertising you that even trees do not die without a groan. It rushes to embrace the earth, and mingle its elements with the dust. And now all is still once more and forever, both to eye and ear.

I went down and measured it. It was about four feet in diameter where it was sawed, about one hundred feet long. Before I had reached it the axemen had already half divested it of its branches. Its gracefully spreading top was a perfect wreck on the hillside as if it had been made of glass, and the tender cones of one year's growth upon its summit appealed in vain and too late to the mercy of the chopper. Already he has measured it with his axe, and marked off the mill-logs it will make. And the space it occupied in upper air is vacant for the next two centuries. It is lumber. He has laid waste the air. When the fish hawk in the spring revisits the banks of the Musketaquid, he will circle in vain to find his accustomed perch, and the hen-hawk will mourn for the pines lofty enough to protect her brood. A plant which it has taken two centuries to perfect, rising by slow stages into the heavens, had this afternoon ceased to exist. Its sapling top had expanded to this January thaw as the forerunner of summers to come. Why does not the village bell sound a knell? I hear no knell tolled. I see no procession of mourners in the streets, or the woodland aisles. The squirrel has leaped to another tree; the hawk has circled further off, and has now settled upon a new eyrie, but the woodman is preparing [to] lay his axe at the root of that also.

ANTONIO MACHADO

To a Withered Elm

On an old elm, rotten in its center
and by a bolt of lightning split,
with the rains of April and the sun of May,
some green leaves have appeared.

The century-old elm on the hill
that the waters of the Duero touch!
A moss stains yellow the whitish bark
of the worm-eaten, dusty trunk.

Unlike the singing poplar trees
that guard the road and the bank,
it won't house brown nightingales.

In a single file an army of ants
bores through it, and in its entrails
the spiders weave their gray web.

Before the Woodsman chops you down,
old elm on the Duero, and the carpenter
puts you to use in a belltower,
or as a wagon axle or yoke;
before red in the fireplace, tomorrow,
you lie burning in some miserable hut

standing by the side of the road;
before a whirlwind uproots you
and the mountain blast breaks you;
before the river pushes you to the sea
through valleys and ravines,
old elm, I want to note
the grace of your leafy limb.
My heart too looks in hope
towards light and life
for another miracle of spring.

Translated by Betty Jean Craige

ANTHONY RYE

Long Lyth Beeches

Tall grow the young trees in the pleasant places
Shielded, their space is, by green living walls
    Parent boughs far sweeping
    Curb the nettles creeping
But all that is altered when a great tree falls

When a great tree which long aloft has lorded
Crashes to the sword it protected and adorned
    Comes the usurping thicket,
    The mean stemmed, the crooked
The squalid, the long buried, the ice-secret-spawned

But more than this—oh still more disenchanted!
Where the long sunray slanted through solemn and still halls
    All now is desolation
And nothing keeps it wooded station—
Oh, but all is altered, altered and forever
    When a great tree falls!

JOHN STEWART COLLIS

FROM *The Worm Forgives the Plough*

On a day in May I sat beside a chestnut tree. It displayed a magnificent show of flowers and when the breeze blew, the petals floated down quite startlingly like a shower of snow. The tree was very large and old. I went and stood under it. A massive trunk. The few holes in the thick canopy of leaves looked like blue stars. I do not think anything in Nature is more mysterious or more effective than a big tree. It is not only that so much proceeds from so little, though this aspect of it is as a supreme exemplar of Nature's method of turning thin air into hard and lofty substance. There is something more about a great tree. Standing under this one and looking up with knitted concentration, quite baffled, I got the impression that it emanated—goodness—It stood there firmly like a noble Thought, which if understood would save the world.

ALDOUS HUXLEY

The Olive Tree

Most of the great deciduous trees of England give one the impression at any rate in summer of being rather obese. In Scandinavia mythology Embla—the elm—was the first woman. Those who have lived much with old elm trees—and I spent a good part of my boyhood under their ponderous shade—will agree that the Scandinavians were men of insight. There is in effect something blowsily female about those vast trees that brood with all their bulging masses of foliage above the meadows of the home counties. In winter they are giant skeletons and for a moment in the early spring a cloud of transparent emerald vapour floats in the air but by June they have settled down to an enormous middle age. . . .

Everywhere and before the world was finally laicized, at all times trees have been worshiped. It is not to be wondered at. The tree is an intrinsically "numinous" being. Solidified—a great fountain of life rises in the trunk—spreads in the branches, scatters in a spray of leaves and flowers and fruits. With a slow silent ferocity, the roots go burrowing down into the earth. Tender yet irresistible life battles with the unliving stones and has the mastery. Half hidden in the darkness, half displayed in the air of heaven, the tree stands there magnificent—a manifest of God. . . .

Even today we feel its majesty and beauty—feel in certain circumstances its rather fearful quality of otherness, strangeness, hostility. Trees in the mass can be almost terrible. There are devils in the great pinewoods of the North, in the swarming equatorial jungle. Alone in the forest one sometimes becomes aware of the silence of the trees. One realizes one's isolation in the midst of a vast concourse of alien presences. Alone or in small groups, trees are benignly numinous. Tamed and isolated those leaping fountains of nonhuman life bring only refreshment to spirits parched by the dusty commerce of the world. . . .

I like them all, but especially the olive, for what it symbolizes—first of all peace with its leaves and joy with its golden oil. True the crown of olive was originally worn by Roman conquerors at ovation. The peace it proclaimed was the peace of victory which is too often only the tranquility of exhaustion of complete annihilation. Rome and its customs have passed and we remember of the olive only the fact that it stood for peace.

ROBERT FROST

Christmas Trees

The city had withdrawn into itself
And left at last the country to the country;
When between whirls of snow not come to lie
And whirls of foliage not yet laid, there drove
A stranger to our yard, who looked the city,
Yet did in country fashion in that there
He sat and waited till he drew us out,
A-buttoning coats, to ask him who he was.
He proved to be the city come again
To look for something it had left behind
And could not do without and keep its Christmas.
He asked if I would sell my Christmas trees.
I doubt if I was tempted for a moment
To sell them off their feet to go in cars
And leave the slope behind the house all bare,
Where the sun shines now no warmer than the moon.
I'd hate to have them know it if I was.
Yet more I'd hate to hold my trees, except
As others hold theirs or refuse for them,
Beyond the time of profitable growth—
The trial by market everything must come to.
I dallied so much with the thought of selling.
Then whether from mistaken courtesy
And fear of seeming short of speech or whether

From hope of hearing good of what was mine,
I said, "There aren't enough to be worth while."

"I could soon tell how many they would cut,
You let me look them over."
                              "You could look.
But don't expect I'm going to let you have them."
Pasture they spring in, some in clumps too close
That lop each other of boughs, but not a few
Quite solitary and having equal boughs
All round and round. The latter he nodded "Yes" to,
Or paused to say beneath some lovelier one, with a
buyer's moderation, "That would do."
I thought so too, but wasn't there to say so.
We climbed the pasture on the south, crossed over,
And came down on the north.
                              He said, "A thousand."
"A thousand Christmas trees!—at what apiece?"

He felt some need of softening that to me:
"A thousand trees would come to thirty dollars."
Then I was certain I had never meant
To let him have them. Never show surprise!
But thirty dollars seemed so small beside
The extent of pasture I should strip, three cents
(For that was all they figured out apiece)—
Three cents so small beside the dollar friends
I should be writing to within the hour
Would pay in cities for good trees like those,
Regular vestry-trees whole Sunday Schools
Could hang enough on to pick off enough.

A thousand Christmas trees I didn't know I had!

TREES

Worth three cents more to give away than sell,
As may be shown by a simple calculation.
Too bad I couldn't lay one in a letter.
I can't help wishing I could send you one
In wishing you herewith a Merry Christmas.

HERMANN HESSE

The Peach Tree

Last night our spring storm, the Fohn, swept mightily and pitilessly over the patient land, across the empty land, across the empty fields and gardens, through the barren vineyards and the barren forest, plucking at every branch and trunk, howling and hissing at everything in its way, making the fig tree rattle like dry bones, and driving whirling clouds of dead leaves high into the air. In the morning great heaps of them lay neatly arranged, subdued and pressed flat, behind every corner and projecting wall that offered shelter from the wind.

And when I went into the garden I found that a catastrophe had occurred. There on the ground lay the largest of my peach trees, broken off close to the earth and pitched over the steep slope of my vineyard. They do not grow to be very old these trees, they do not belong among the giants and heroes, they are delicate and susceptible, overly sensitive to injury, their resinous sap has something of ancient, too highly bred blood lines. It was not an especially beautiful or noble tree, the one that had fallen there, but it was, after all, the largest of my peach trees, an old acquaintance and friend, a resident older than I on these acres. Each year soon after the middle of March it had opened its buds and dramatically displayed its rosy foam of blossoms against the blue of a fair-weather sky and infinitely delicate against stormy heavens, it had shuddered in the capricious squalls of the fresh April days, burnished by the golden flames of brimstone butterflies; it had braced itself against the evil Fohn, had stood silent and as though dreaming in the wet gray of the rainy times, bending slightly to gaze toward its feet where with each day of rain the grass on the steep vineyard slope grew greener and lusher. Sometimes I had taken one of its small blooming twigs into the house with me; occasionally when its fruit began to be too heavy I had helped it out with a prop; also in earlier years I had been audacious enough to try to paint it when it was in bloom. At every time of year since I had lived here, it had had its place in my small world and I belonged to it, it shared with me heat and snow, storm and quietude, had added its tone to the song, its resonance to the picture; it had gradually grown high above the vine props and had outlived generations of lizards, snakes, butterflies, and birds. It was not remarkable, it had not been highly regarded, but it had been indispensable. When the fruit began to ripen I would make the small excursion every morning from the stairway over to it and pick up out of the wet grass the peaches that had fallen during the night and bring them back in my pockets, in a basket, or sometimes in my hat and set them on the railing of the terrace.

Now at the spot that had belonged to this old acquaintance and friend there was an empty place. The small world had a tear in it through which the void, darkness, death, terror looked in. The broken trunk lay there sadly, its wood looking soft and a little spongy. The limbs had been broken in the fall; in two weeks perhaps they would have once more worn their rosy-red spring crowns and held them up to the blue of the gray of the skies. Never again would I pluck a twig, never again gather a fruit from it, never again would I attempt to draw the capricious and somewhat fantastic structure of its spreading branches, never again on a hot summer day would I stroll over from the steps to rest for a moment in its lacy shade. I called Lorenzo the gardener and instructed him to carry the fallen tree to the barn. There, on the first rainy day when there was no other work to be done, it would be sawed up for firewood. Indignantly I watched him depart. To think that you couldn't rely even on trees, they too could slip away from you, could die, one day they could leave you in the lurch and disappear into the great darkness!

I gazed after Lorenzo, who was having trouble pulling the heavy trunk. Farewell, my dear peach tree! At least you died a decent, natural, and proper death and for this I call you happy; you braced yourself and held out as long as you possibly could and then the great enemy wrenched your limbs from their sockets. You had to give way, you fell and were severed from your roots. You were not splintered by bombs from the air, not burnt by hellish acids, not, like millions, torn from your native earth, hastily replanted with bleeding roots, only to be seized anew and rendered homeless once more, you have not had to experience catastrophe and destruction, war and degradation around you or been forced to die in misery. You have had a fate such as become and is due to your kind. For this I call you blessed; you grew older better and more gracefully than we and you died with greater dignity than we who in our day must defend ourselves against the poison and the misery of a polluted world, must fight against encompassing corrosive corruption for every breath of clean air.

When I had seen the tree lying there, I had thought of a replacement, another tree to plant, as is usual with such losses. Where it had fallen we would dig a hole and let it stand open for a good while, exposed to the rain and wind and sun; into the hole we would after a while put some fertilizer, some dung from the compost heaps and all sorts of wood ash mixed with scraps, and then one day, if possible when a soft mild rain was falling, we would plant a new young small tree. Earth and air here would be completely to the liking of this newcomer, too, this child tree, it too would become a comrade and good neighbor to the vines, the flowers, the lizards, the birds, and the butterflies, in a few years it would bear fruit every spring in the second half of March would produce its lovely blossoms and, if the fates were favorable, one day as an old and weary tree would fall victim to some storm or landslide or the heaviness of the snow.

But this time I could not make up my mind to replant. I had set out a good many trees in my lifetime; this single one did not matter. And there was something within me that resisted renewing the cycle here at this place, giving another push to the wheel of life, nurturing a new prey for ravenous death. I do not want to do it. The place shall remain empty.

Translated by Denver Lindley

A. E. HOUSMAN

FROM *A Shropshire Lad*

Loveliest of trees, the cherry now
Is hung with bloom along the bough.
And stands about the woodland ride
Wearing white for Eastertide.

Now of my threescore years and ten,
Twenty will not come again.
And take from seventy springs a score,
It only leaves me fifty more.

And since to look at things in bloom
Fifty springs are little room.
About the woodlands I will go
To see the cherry hung with snow.

ANTONIO MACHADO

To an Orange Tree and a Lemon Tree Seen in a Plant and Flower Store

Orange tree in a flower pot, how sad is your fate!
Your withered leaves shiver with fear.
Orange trees in Madrid, what sorrow to see you
with your little oranges, dry and wrinkled!

Poor lemon tree with yellow fruit
like polished apples of pale wax,
What sorrow to look at you, wretched little tree,
raised in a miserable wooden barrel!

From the bright green groves of Andalusia,
who brought you, children of my native
land, to this Castilian plain
swept by the winds of the grim sierra?

Glory of the orchards, O lemon tree,
kindling your pale golden fruit,
and illuminating the quiet prayers
of the stern black cypresses in chorus raised;

and fresh orange tree of the beloved patio,
of the smiling countryside and the orchard of my dreams,
always in my memory, ripe or in flower,
laden with fronds and aromas and fruit!

Translated by Richard L. Predmore

PIERRE DE RONSARD

Ode

Beautiful hawthorn tree in flower
    Your green bower
Stretches along the river's edge;
And you are dressed from head to foot,
    With twisted root,
In a wild and thorny hedge.

Red ants swarm upon the ground
    All around
At your feet in brightest red;

Pierre de Ronsard

In the tangle of your boughs
    Birds soon rouse
Morning from their leafy bed

Here the nightingale doth sing
    And yearly bring
To his mate a lover's vow.
Wooing so where she doth dwell
    With magic spell
From the highest hawthorn bough

In thy treetop he has made,
    All arrayed
A nest of silken moss, and gay;
Whence the nestlings soon will fly
    By and by
In my clasp a gentle prey

Live, then gentle hawthorn, live!
    May fate find
Life unending, thunderless!
Neither axe nor keenest blast
    Thee at last
Tear down in harsh bitterness.

Translated by William Stirling

JOHANN WOLFGANG VON GOETHE

FROM *Goethe's World View*

Our destiny sometimes has the appearance of a fruit tree in winter. Looking at its dreary aspect, who would think that these stiff branches, these jagged twigs, will turn green again and bloom next spring and then bear fruit. Yet this we hope, this we know.

Translated by Heinz Norden

ROBERT FROST

Birches

When I see birches bend to left and right
Across the lines of straighter darker trees,
I like to think some boy's been swinging them.
But swinging doesn't bend them down to stay
As ice storms do. Often you must have seen them
Loaded with ice a sunny winter morning
After a rain. They click upon themselves
As the breeze rises, and turn many-colored

As the stir cracks and crazes their enamel.
Soon the sun's warmth makes them shed crystal shells
Shattering and avalanching on the snow crust—
Such heaps of broken glass to sweep away
You'd think the inner dome of heaven had fallen.
They are dragged to the withered bracken by the load,
And they seem not break; though once they are bowed
So low for long, they never right themselves:
You may see their trunks arching in the woods
Years afterwards, trailing their leaves on the ground
Like girls on hands and knees that throw their hair
Before them over their heads to dry in the sun.
But I was going to say when Truth broke in
With all her matter of fact about the ice storm,
I should prefer to have some boy bend them
As he went out and in to fetch the cows—
Some boy too far from town to learn baseball,
Whose only play was what he found himself,
Summer or winter, and could play alone.
One by one he subdued his father's trees
By riding them down over and over again
Until he took the stiffness out of them,
And not one but hung limp, not one was left
For him to conquer. He learned all there was
To learn about not launching out too soon
And so not carrying the tree away
Clear to the ground. He always kept his poise
To the top branches, climbing carefully
With the same pains you use to fill a cup
Up to the brim, and even about the brim.
Then he flung outward, feet first, with a swish,
Kicking his way down through the air to the ground.
So was I once myself a swinger of birches.

And so I dream of going back to be.
It's when I'm weary of considerations,
And life is too much like a pathless wood
Where your face burns and tickles with the cobwebs
Broken across it, and one eye is weeping
From a twig's having lashed across it open.
I'd like to get away from earth awhile
And then come back to it and begin over.
May no fate willfully understand me
And half grant what I wish and snatch me away
Not to return. Earth's the right place for love:
I don't know where it's likely to go better.
I'd like to go by climbing a birch tree,
And climb black branches up a snow-white trunk
Toward heaven, till the tree could bear no more,
But dipped its top and set me down again.
That would be good both going and coming back.
One could do worse than be a swinger of birches.

HANS CHRISTIAN ANDERSEN

The Fir-Tree

Far away in the deep forest there once grew a pretty Fir-Tree; the situation was delightful, the sun shone full upon him, the breeze played freely around him, and in the neighbourhood grew many companion fir-trees, some older, some younger. But the little Fir-Tree was not happy: he was always longing to be tall; he thought not of the warm sun and the fresh air; he cared not for the merry, prattling peasant children who came to the forest to look for strawberries and raspberries. Except, indeed, sometimes, when, after having filled their pitchers, or threaded the bright berries on a straw, they would sit down near the little Fir-Tree, and say, "What a pretty little tree this is!" and then the Fir-Tree would feel very much vexed.

Year by year he grew, a long green shoot sent he forth every year; for you may always tell how many years a fir-tree has lived by counting the number of joints in its stem.

"Oh, that I was as tall as the others are," sighed the little Tree, "then I should spread out my branches so far, and my crown should look out over the wide world around! The birds would build their nests among my branches, and when the wind blew I should bend my head so grandly, just as the others do!"

He had no pleasure in the sunshine, in the song of the birds, or in the red clouds that sailed over him every morning and evening.

In the winter-time, when the ground was covered with the white, glistening snow, there was a hare that would come continually scampering about, and jumping right over the little Tree's head—and that was most provoking! However, two winters passed away, and by the third the Tree was so tall that the hare was obliged to run round it. "Oh! to grow, to grow, to become tall and old, that is the only thing in the world worth living for"—so thought the Tree.

The wood-cutters came in the autumn and felled some among the largest of the trees; this happened every year, and our young Fir, who was by this time a tolerable height, shuddered when he saw those grand, magnificent trees fall with a tremendous crash, crackling to the earth: their boughs were then all cut off; terribly naked, and lanky, and long did the stems look after this—they could hardly be recognised. They were laid one upon another in waggons, and horses drew them away, far, far away, from the forest. Where could they be going? What might be their fortunes?

So next spring, when the Swallows and the Storks had returned from abroad, the Tree asked them, saying, "Know you not whither they are taken? Have you not met them?"

The Swallows knew nothing about the matter, but the Stork looked thoughtful for a moment, then nodded his head, and said, "Yes, I believe I have seen them! As I was flying from Egypt to this place I met several ships; those ships had splendid masts. I have little doubt that they were the trees that you speak of; they smelled like fir-wood. I may congratulate you, for they sailed gloriously, quite gloriously!"

"Oh, that I, too, were tall enough to sail upon the sea! Tell me what it is, this sea, and what it looks like."

"Thank you, it would take too long, a great deal!" said the Stork, and away he stalked.

"Rejoice in thy youth!" said the Sunbeams; "rejoice in thy luxuriant youth, in the fresh life that is within thee!"

And the Wind kissed the Tree, and the Dew wept tears over him, but the Fir-Tree understood them not.

When Christmas approached, many quite young trees were felled—trees which were some of them not so tall or of just the same height as the young restless Fir-Tree who was always longing to be away; these young trees were chosen from the most beautiful, their branches were not cut off, they were laid on a waggon, and horses drew them away, far, far away, from the forest. I suffer, I suffer with longing! I know not what it is that I feel!"

"Rejoice in our love!" said the Air and the Sunshine. "Rejoice in thy youth and thy freedom!"

But rejoice he never would: he grew and grew, in winter as in summer; he stood there clothed in green, dark-green foliage; the people that saw him, said, "That is a beautiful tree!" and, next Christmas, he was the first that was felled. The axe struck sharply through the wood, the tree fell to the earth with a heavy groan; he suffered an agony, a faintness that he had never expected; he quite forgot to think of his good fortune, he felt such sorrow at being compelled to leave his home, the place whence he had sprung; he knew that he should never see again those dear old comrades, or the little bushes and the flowers that had flourished under his shadow, perhaps not even the birds. Neither did he find the journey by any means pleasant.

The Tree first came to himself when, in the courtyard to which he was first taken with the other trees, he heard a man say, "This is a splendid one, the very thing we want!"

Then came two smartly-dressed servants, and carried the Fir-Tree into a large and handsome saloon. Pictures hung on the walls, and on the mantelpiece stood large Chinese vases with lions on the lids; there were rocking-chairs, silken sofas, tables covered with picture-books, and toys that had cost a hundred times a hundred dollars—at least so said the children. And the Fir-Tree was planted in a large cask filled with sand, but no one could know that it was a cask, for it was hung with green cloth and placed upon a carpet woven of many gay colours. Oh, how the Tree trembled! What was to happen next? A young lady, assisted by the servants, now began to adorn him.

Upon some branches they hung little nets cut out of coloured paper, every net filled with sugar-plums; from other gilded apples and walnuts were suspended, looking just as if they had grown there; and more than a hundred little wax-tapers, red, blue, and white, were placed here and there among the boughs. Dolls, that looked almost like men and women— the Tree had never seen such things before—seemed dancing to and fro among the leaves, and highest, on the summit, was fastened a large star of gold tinsel; this was, indeed, splendid, splendid beyond compare! "This evening," they said, "this evening it will be lighted up."

"Would that it were evening?" thought the Tree. "Would that the lights were kindled, for then—what will happen then? Will the trees come out of the forest to see me? Will the sparrows fly here and look in through the window-panes? Shall I stand here adorned both winter and summer?"

He thought much of it; he thought till he had bark-ache with longing, and bark-aches with trees are as bad as headaches with us. The candles were lighted—oh, what a blaze of splendour! The Tree trembled in all his branches, so that one of them caught fire. "Oh, dear!" cried the young lady, and it was extinguished in great haste.

So the Tree dared not tremble again; he was so fearful of losing something of his splendour, he felt almost bewildered in the midst of all this glory and brightness. And now, all of a sudden, both folding-doors were flung open, and a troop of children rushed in as if they had a mind to jump over him; the older people followed more quietly; the little ones stood quite silent, but only for a moment! Then their jubilee burst forth afresh; they shouted till the walls re-echoed, they danced round the Tree, one present after another was torn down.

"What are they doing?" thought the Tree; "what will happen now?" And the candles burned down to the branches, so they were extinguished—and the children were given leave to plunder the Tree. Oh! they rushed upon him such riot that the boughs all crackled; had not his summit been festooned with the gold star to the ceiling he would have been over-turned.

The children danced and played about with their beautiful playthings, no one thought any more of the Tree except the old nurse, who came and peeped among the boughs, but it was only to see whether perchance a fig or an apple had not been left among them.

"A story! A story!" cried the children, pulling a short thick man towards the tree. He sat down, saying, "It is pleasant to sit under the shade of green boughs; besides, the Tree may be benefited by hearing my story. But I shall only tell you one. Would you like to hear about Ivedy Avedy, or about Humpty Dumpty, who fell downstairs, and yet came to the throne and won the Princess?"

"Ivedy Avedy!" cried some. "Humpty Dumpty!" cried

others; there was a famous uproar; the Fir-Tree along was silent, thinking to himself, "Ought I to make a noise as they do, or ought I to do nothing at all?" for he most certainly was one of the company, and had done all that had been required of him.

And the short thick man told the story of Humpty Dumpty, who fell downstairs, and yet came to the throne and won the Princess. And the children clapped their hands and called out for another; they wanted to hear the story of Ivedy Avedy also, but they did not get it. The Fir-Tree stood meanwhile quite silent and thoughtful—the birds in the forest had never related anything like this. "Humpty Dumpty fell downstairs, and yet was raised to the throne and won the Princess! Yes, yes, strange things come to pass in the world!" thought the Fir-Tree, who believed it must all be true, because such a pleasant man had related it. "Ah, ah! Who knows but I may fall downstairs and win a Princess?" And he rejoiced in the expectation of being next day again decked out with candles and playthings, gold and fruit.

"To-morrow I will not tremble," thought he. "I will rejoice in my magnificence. To-morrow I shall again hear the story of Humpty Dumpty, and perhaps that about Ivedy Avedy likewise." And the Tree mused thereupon all night.

In the morning the maids came in.

"Now begins my state anew!" thought the Tree. But they dragged him out of the room, up the stairs, and into an attic-chamber, and there thrust him into a dark corner, where not a ray of light could penetrate. "What can be the meaning of this?" thought the Tree. "What am I to do here? What shall I hear in this place?" and he leant against the wall, and thought, and thought. And plenty of time he had for thinking it over, for day after day, and night after night, passed away, and yet no one ever came into the room. At last somebody did come in, but it was only to push into the corner some old trunks: the Tree was now entirely hidden from sight, and apparently entirely forgotten.

"It is now winter," thought the Tree. "The ground is hard and covered with snow; they cannot plant me now, so I am to stay here in shelter till the spring. Men are so clever and prudent! I only wish it were not so dark and so dreadfully lonely! Not even a little hare! Oh, how pleasant it was in the forest, when the snow lay on the ground the hare scampered about—yes, even when he jumped over my head, though I did not like it then. It is so terribly lonely here."

"Squeak! Squeak!" cried a little Mouse, just then gliding forward. Another followed; they snuffed about the Fir-Tree, and then slipped in and out among the branches.

"It is horribly cold!" said the little Mice. "Otherwise it is very comfortable here. Don't you think so, you old Fir-tree?"

"I am not old," said the Fir-Tree; "there are many who are much older than I am."

"How came you here?" asked the Mice, "and what do you know?" They were most uncommonly curious. "Tell us about the most delightful place on earth! Have you ever been there? Have you been in the store-room, where cheeses lie on the shelves, and bacon hangs from the ceiling; where one can dance over tallow-candles; where one goes in thin and comes out fat?"

"I know nothing about that," said the Tree, "but I know the forest, where the sun shines and where the birds sing!" and then he spoke of his youth and its pleasure. The little Mice had never heard anything like it before; they listened so attentively and said, "Well, to be sure! How much you have seen! How happy you have been!"

"Happy!" repeated the Fir-Tree, in surprise, and he thought a moment over all that he had been saying—"Yes, on the whole, those were pleasant times!" He then told them about the Christmas Eve, when he had been decked out with cakes and candles.

"Oh!" cried the little Mice, "how happy you have been, you old Fir-Tree!"

"I am not old at all!" returned the Fir; "it is only this winter that I have left the forest; I am just in the prime of life!"

"How well you can talk!" said the little Mice; and the next night they came again, and brought with them four other little Mice, who wanted also to hear the Tree's history; and the more the Tree spoke of his youth in the forest, the more vividly he remembered it, and said, "Yes, those were pleasant times! But they may come again, they may come again! Humpty Dumpty fell downstairs, and for all that he won the Princess; perhaps I, too, may win a Princess"; and then the Fir-Tree thought of a pretty little delicate Birch-Tree that grew in the forest—a real Princess, a very lovely Princess, was she to the Fir-Tree.

"Who is this Humpty Dumpty?" asked the little Mice. Whereupon he related the tale; he could remember every word of it perfectly: and the little Mice were ready to jump to the top of the Tree for joy. The night following several more Mice came, and on Sunday came also two Rats; they, however, declared that the story was not at all amusing, which much vexed the little Mice, who, after hearing their opinion, could not like it so well either.

"Do you know only that one story?" asked the Rats.

"Only that one!" answered the Tree; "I heard it on the happiest evening of my life, though I did not then know how happy it was."

"It is a miserable story! Do you know none about pork and tallow? —no store-room story?"

"No," said the Tree.

"Well, then we have heard enough of it!" returned the Rats, and they went their ways.

The little Mice, too, never came again. The Tree sighed. "It was pleasant when they sat round me, those busy little Mice, listening to my words. Now that, too, is all past! However, I shall have pleasure in remembering it, when I am taken away from this place."

But when would that be? One morning, people came and routed out the lumber-room; the trunks were taken away, the Tree, too, was dragged out of the corner; they threw him carelessly on the floor, but one of the servants picked him up and carried him downstairs. Once more he beheld the light of day.

"Now life begins again!" thought the Tree; he felt the fresh air, the warm sunbeams—he was out in the court. All happened so quickly that the Tree quite forgot to look at himself—there was so much to look at all around. The court joined a garden, everything was so fresh and blooming, the roses clustered so bright and so fragrant round the trellis-work, the lime-trees were in full blossom, and the swallows flew backwards and forwards, twittering, "Quirri-virri-vit, my beloved is come!" but it was not the Fir-Tree whom they meant.

"I shall live! I shall live!" He was filled with delightful hope; he tried to spread out his branches, but, alas! they were all dried up and yellow. He was thrown down upon a heap of weeds and nettles. The star of gold tinsel that had been left fixed on his crown now sparked brightly in the sunshine.

Some merry children were playing in the court, the same who at Christmas-time had danced round the Tree. One of the youngest now perceived the gold star, and ran to tear it off.

"Look at it, still fastened to the ugly old Christmas-

Tree!" cried he, trampling upon the boughs till they broke under his boots.

And the Tree looked on all the flowers of the garden now blooming in the freshness of their beauty; he looked upon himself and he wished from his heart that he had been left to wither alone in the dark corner of the lumber-room: he called to mind his happy forest-life, the merry Christmas Eve, and the little Mice who had listened so eagerly when he related the story of Humpty Dumpty.

"Past, all past!" said the poor Tree. "Had I but been happy, as I might have been! Past, all past!"

And the servant came and broke the Tree into small pieces, heaped them up and set fire to them. And the Tree groaned deeply, and every groan sounded like a little shot; the children all ran up the place and jumped about in front of the blaze, looking into it and crying, "Piff! piff!" But at each of those heavy groans the Fir-Tree thought of a bright summer's day, on a starry winter's night in the forest, of Christmas Eve, or of Humpty Dumpty, the only story that he knew and could relate. And at last the Tree was burned.

The boys played about in the court; on the bosom of the youngest sparkled the gold star that the Tree had worn on the happiest evening of his life; but that was past, and the Tree was past, and the story also, past! past! for all stories must come to an end, some time or another.